WARRIOR MOM

How I Fought To Get A Great Education and Scholarships For My Children and Others

RHONDA COPELAND LYLE

Copyright ©2020 Rhonda Copeland Lyle

ISBN: 979-8-218-01216-8

Author: Rhonda Copeland Lyle
Editor: Valerie L. McDowell
Cover Design: Daniel O. Ojedokun
Layout: Velin@Perseus-Design.com
Publisher: Power2Excel

Printed in the United States of America.

ALL RIGHTS RESERVED. This book contains material protected under international and federal copyright laws and treaties. Any unauthorized reprint or use of this material is prohibited. No part of this book may be reproduced or transmitted in any form or by any means, electronic or mechanical, including photocopying, recording, or by any information storage and retrieval system without express written permission from the author: Rhondalyle411@gmail.com

DEDICATION

This book is dedicated to my mother, Marguerite "Peggy" Copeland (1936-1988), the inspiration for my life. She was a single mother who sacrificed so much for her children. Although she did not attend college, she encouraged me to get my degree. This book is a tribute to her and to what education can do in the life of a child. My mother was relentless in her pursuit for getting things accomplished in spite of obstacles. She never gave up. I am my mother's daughter.

Original Artwork by Danielle Marguerite Lyle

CONTENTS

ACKNOWLEDGEMENT	vii
INTRODUCTION	1
CHAPTER ONE: How It All Began	5
CHAPTER TWO: How I Became an Activist for My Children's Education	15
CHAPTER THREE: The Right Path	25
CHAPTER FOUR: It Starts at Home	29
CHAPTER FIVE: When Young People Take the Lead	61
CHAPTER SIX: World Travel	63
CHAPTER SEVEN: Don't Let A Disability Diminish Expectations of What Your Child Can Accomplish	69
CHAPTER EIGHT: Do Everything You Can to Help Your Child Succeed	75
CHAPTER NINE: Be Your Child's Best Advocate	79
CHAPTER TEN: Conclusion	83
SOME LETTERS OF RECOMMENDATIONS OVER THE YEARS	85
EPILOGUE	97
A SHORT LISTING OF OPPORTUNITIES FOR STUDENTS	99
A NOTE FROM THE AUTHOR	103

ACKNOWLEDGEMENT

This book acknowledges all of the parents, guardians, friends, colleagues, and anyone who knows the difficulty in acquiring the best education possible for children, with funding. This is to all the parents who have had to fight closed quotas, unknown requirements, private conversations, and any roadblock—seen or unseen—that have limited what their children can do when given the opportunity.

This book is for the average family with limited funds who could never dream that these opportunities are available to their children, either for free or at limited cost.

Inside these pages you will gain a wealth of information to transform the lives of your children and give them opportunities outside the status quo of what is available for most children.

Finally, this book is a labor of love—a labor of finding the best resources, opportunities, schools, and programs here in the United States and all over the world for your child, no matter their ability or different ability.

This is my gift to you.

INTRODUCTION

For the last 20 years I have researched fun, educational enrichment programs and scholarships that my children, their friends and others participated in – many at no or minimal cost. If there was a substantial cost, I was able to negotiate a lesser cost, even when I was told it could not be done.

During this period, I assisted families in obtaining more than 10 million in scholarship dollars, not only for my children, but for other students as well. This included scholarships for private middle and high schools, travel abroad, and worldwide academic/enrichment programs like leadership programs in New York, California, and Congressional programs in Washington, DC and abroad.

The principles and information in this book apply whether your child is in the United States or in another country, no matter what stage in school they are in.

I have been an invited speaker at churches, sororities, social organizations, and other nonprofit events providing parents and students information about these opportunities. This book is the result of many friends asking me to write a book about all the programs I have counseled them through over the years.

I believe in educating students to be global citizens and passionate lifelong learners. I want to see our youth travel the world, in person or virtually, to experience other people, other cultures, and share the average American life in the United States. I am not referring to just the headlines, which do not represent most Americans. I believe the world is our playground, our classroom. Take advantage of it, get out and see it, and experience it through peace, love, and humanity.

Warrior:
a noun that refers to a soldier or someone who is involved in a fight. Today, the word warrior is frequently used to describe a person who is strong and doesn't give up easily

- MacMillion Dictionary

CHAPTER ONE

HOW IT ALL BEGAN

Education is the key to success in today's global world. I realized this in sixth grade when I won an award for reading 100 books during the school year. The requirement was that each student read two to three books during the year and then they would have a discussion about the books in class.

After reading the first book, I asked the teacher if I could take a book home to read. The teacher said yes. I returned the book in two days and asked for another one. I returned that book and asked for yet another one. My teacher asked if I had really read the books. When I said that I had, she asked me questions about them to ensure I had indeed read them. She could not believe I had read a book in two days and she was happy that I wanted to read more.

During the school year I read every book in the teacher's closet: 100 books. I didn't realize I had read that many, as I was not counting the books as I read. They were all about African Americans, many of whom I'd never heard of before.

After the first book, I was hooked on reading. I always had a book in my hand or was at the local library. Reading books opened the world to me.

When my youngest daughter, Danielle, was five years old, I started a book club for her and her friends. She loved to read, and

I wanted her to continue reading. After searching online for book clubs we could join, I only found book clubs for older students. So, I decided to start my own club with her friends and their families. I wanted her to continue her love of reading and more. I wanted her to read about great African Americans.

At the time, she attended the Cardinal Montessori school in Woodbridge, Virginia, a predominantly white school. It was an excellent school and she was able to read a lot there as well as at home. However, I wanted her to read books about people who looked like her. The book club started with five Black students from her school, three to five years old. The requirement was to read books by and about African Americans so the students could explore the riches of their community.

The book club met every quarter. The moms had full-time jobs and, for some, other children and husbands so there were schedules to work around. Parents would take turns hosting a book club meeting and they would select the book the children were to read and schedule an event around the subject of the book. I developed an outline for the parents to follow to ensure the children knew the subject of the book, the main idea, discussion items, conclusions, and their personal comments about the book. Each child had to read their favorite passage from the book to their peers and parents. If they could not yet read, the parent had to read the book to them and help them complete the outline.

This gave the children confidence to speak in public and develop reading and speaking skills in a supportive environment where everyone was cheering them on with love. It gave them confidence. My daughter, Danielle, was also shy, but I wanted to help her grow out of that stage early in life. The children loved the book club and looked forward to meeting and doing activities surrounding the books they read. At the first meeting at my house, we read a book about Martin Luther King, Jr., and had discussions and a presentation about the book. All the children had to participate. We watched a cartoon about MLK with the kids going back in time to meet him. They loved the cartoon as it gave them more of an understanding about what they had read about MLK on a level they could understand at their young ages.

The book club read all kinds of books and participated in various events and activities. They read books about Frederick Douglass and visited the Frederick Douglass house in DC. They read books about cowboys and cooking out on the range then they cooked a delicious meal. The club attended the National Book Festival every year and met authors, purchased books, and were excited to have the authors autograph their books. They went to see the Lion King at the Kennedy Center as well as went to book festivals and the children's play series produced by actress and dancer Debbie Allen. They book club was also invited to meet Supreme Court Justice Sonia Sotomayor and took photos with her.

The book club members were asked to make a special presentation to Princess Ncengencenge (Nancy) Dlamini from Swaziland (the Kingdom of Eswatini in Southern Africa). They had one day to prepare for the presentation. While my daughter and Anisa, who were the older girls in the book club at ages 8 and 9, wrote the presentation for the Princess, two older boys at age 9, Marcus and Kyle, recited a poem they selected. The book club girls wore white gowns (former flower girl dresses from weddings) with crowns and the boys wore black suits and white shirts with black bow ties. All the kids participated in the presentation. They practiced the day before in front of the parents.

On the day of the presentation, they presented a basket of new books to Princess Nancy to take back to the orphanage's children who had lost their parents to HIV/AIDS. Also, they gave the princess a money order for $200 of their own money and made it clear that it was their money and not their parents.

The children participated in the book club from preschool/kindergarten all the way through high school. When they got to middle school, they decided that they wanted to select their own books to read and the activities they would do. As parents we were delighted with this choice. It showed their sense of independence, decision making abilities, and leadership.

During the national campaign for President of the U.S. in 2008, my daughter was 10 years old, and I organized the children, with the book club moms, to present and celebrate President Obama's election win. The children each selected an excerpt to recite from one of the speeches Obama gave on the campaign trail. They all wore red, white, and/or blue. Most of the girls wore white dresses, again. The boys wore navy blue suits with red ties and white shirts. We used one of the parents' clubhouses in their neighborhood, free of charge, and invited the community. The space held 200 people and was full. I sent out a press release to the *Washington Post*, which sent a photographer to cover the event, and the photos from the event appeared on the front page of the local section of the *Post* two days later. I sent a letter to the White House after President Obama's inauguration and the book club children received a letter from President Obama congratulating them on their involvement in the elections and the many hours of community service.

Fast forward four years, the children were now in high school, and President Obama had been re-elected. My daughter and I organized another event, this time at my home to celebrate the president's re-election. We invited State Senator George Barker of Virginia to be our keynote speaker. He accepted and attended. I was also in communication with Patrick Gaspard, President Obama's former political director at the White House and, at the time, the Ambassador to South Africa, to see if he would be available to attend the event. It was a long shot, but I put the request in. He accepted and attended as well.

How It All Began

THE WHITE HOUSE

WASHINGTON

Congratulations on receiving the President's Volunteer Service Award, and thank you for helping to address the most pressing needs in your community and our country.

In my Inaugural Address, I stated that we need a new era of responsibility—a recognition on the part of every American that we have duties to ourselves, our Nation, and the world. These are duties that we do not grudgingly accept, but rather seize gladly, firm in the knowledge that there is nothing so satisfying to the spirit than giving our all to a difficult task. Your volunteer service demonstrates the kind of commitment to your community that moves America a step closer to its great promise.

Our Nation faces the most challenging economic crisis in a lifetime. We will only renew America if we all work together. Individuals, the private sector, and government must combine efforts to make real and lasting change so that each person has the opportunity to fulfill his or her potential.

While government can open more opportunities for us to serve our communities, it is up to each of us to seize those opportunities. Thank you for your devotion to service and for doing all you can to shape a better tomorrow for our great Nation.

The back story to Gaspard was that his sister and her two older daughters were members of the book club. However, she never asked her brother for any favors in his capacity with President Obama or the White House. So, I did not ask her to reach out to him. Instead, I did. I had nothing to lose. There was a 50-50 chance he would say yes, and he did. He asked that I keep his attendance a surprise to his sister and his nieces. They were pleasantly surprised when he arrived, and State Senator George Barker did not mind at all sharing the spotlight with Gaspard. The event concluded with the book club kids doing a round table discussion about the campaign and issues of importance to them. My daughter came up with the topics and included the other children in what they would be. The guests, including Gaspard and State Senator Barker, were impressed with the children – our future leaders – being so involved in the political process and all levels of issues.

Parents can make a difference in their children's school life if they are involved and are willing to speak up for what can benefit not only their child but others as well. You may be surprised by the positive response you get. However, don't be afraid to be a warrior mom or activist parent for your child when necessary. I was able to secure $2 million in scholarships for my three children from elementary school to college. In addition, the daughter of one of the families I assisted, went on to receive $1.4 million in scholarships in 2018 for college.

"Don't just get involved, fight for your seat at the table. Better yet, fight for a seat at the head of the table."
- President Barack Obama

How It All Began

THE WHITE HOUSE
WASHINGTON

April 6, 2009

Future Leaders Youth Book Club

Dear Friends:

Thank you for writing to our family!

Our daughters are happily settling into their new surroundings and routines. They're having fun making new friends and working hard on their homework. The girls really enjoy living in the White House and discovering the history that surrounds them in our new home. The White House is a place that all Americans should treasure and enjoy. You can learn more about the White House and take an online tour at www.whitehousehistory.org. It's not just our house – it's your house too!

Right now is a special time for our family, but it is also an important moment in our country's history. Many people have worked hard to make the United States what it is today, and I hope you know that you can play a big role in its future, too. I encourage you to talk to your family or teacher about ways to help in your community. Just a little volunteer time can really help one of your neighbors.

Thanks again for writing. I appreciate how hard you worked on your letter. Keep up the good work!

Sincerely,

Michelle Obama

White House letter to the book club

The Future Leaders Book Club kids, ages 3-5 years old.

Future Leaders Book Club members in High School

CHAPTER TWO

HOW I BECAME AN ACTIVIST FOR MY CHILDREN'S EDUCATION

"The only limit to your success is your imagination."
- Shonda Rhimes

Precisely what is an activist parent? It is a parent fighting for their child's education and demanding excellence from educational systems.

The initial responsibility begins in the home. I demanded and expected excellence from each of my children according to their ability. Each child is a unique individual. My rules for everyone during the school day: no watching TV, videos, phones, texting, or computer use unless it is to work on a school project. Have a set bedtime during the school year, unless you feel your child has proven to be responsible enough to set their own bedtime and be ready for classes and alert the next day.

As parents, we have the responsibility to teach and educate our children. This should be done in coordination with their teachers when possible. If you think your children are not getting what they need academically, find outside programs for them to participate in.

Communicate with teachers. Do not be intimidated by teachers or administrators. Let the teachers know via email and conversation that you will be involved in your child's academic success and school life and will work with them as a partner.

"Don't have a defeatist attitude when things get hard. Don't become apathetic. You will have to do the work."
~Rhonda C. Lyle

A child is no match when dealing with a teacher who is not cooperating with a request from the child or parent. The teacher holds all the cards, and you do not want the teacher to brush off the child. Start by always being courteous with the teacher to get what you want. If that doesn't work, go over their head to the school administrators. Also, always put your requests in writing. The email trail may prove useful at a later date. Make an appointment with the teacher and/or visit the school and wait to talk to the teacher or administrators until your request is granted. I was an alpha mom and proud of it. After a while, the teachers welcomed my involvement and sought me out.

I do believe children should learn early how to advocate for themselves and speak up in a respectful way. However, as soon as a teacher is dismissive with the child, as a parent, you must step up and step in.

How To Get Your Child Off To A Great Start

Over the years, I have found the following tips to be helpful as my children matriculated through their school years. I often offer these tips to other families.

1. Send an email to meet with all teachers at the beginning of the school year. Tell them about your child, your expectations of your child and the teacher. Let the teacher know you want to partner with them to ensure your child's success at school.
2. Follow-up with an email to all teachers, counselors, and administrators. This will ensure you are all working from the same playbook.
3. Set expectations early with the teacher and for your child.
4. When you ask a teacher to complete a recommendation for your child, write a suggested letter about your child to assist the teacher in writing it with a minimum amount of effort. Many teachers are too busy to write a recommendation and will appreciate you making it easy for them to complete in a timely manner. They might have up to 32 children in their classroom and may not always remember each accomplishment.
5. Schedule activities with your children's friends to have fun while learning. It helps them stay engaged and doing things with friends takes the pressure off parents in making their children do certain activities.
6. Find a teacher or school staff person to work in partnership with you to provide information about opportunities for your child, and who will let you know if your child is doing something that needs to stop.

NOTE: The easier you make it for teachers to help your child, the better off everyone will be. Don't make their job more difficult or add more to their plate then they already have, when it benefits your child.

Explore All Options

I met the Gifted Education Superintendent of Schools from a school district outside of my designated area at an event. He mentioned that he was hosting a Mensa event for teachers and school administrators of gifted programs in his school district. Mensa is an international society with the only qualification for membership being a high IQ. Generally, a 12-year-old with an IQ of 120 can be eligible to join Mensa for kids. Mensa is for folks from all walks of life, from a truck driver to millionaires. The speaker wanted to encourage school faculty to consider minority students for Mensa if they were only 2-3 points below the Mensa IQ requirement. I crashed the workshop and drove in the notorious Washington, DC traffic from Virginia to attend the event. Of course, I was the only non-teacher/administrator there.

The speaker talked about the need to encourage participation of gifted minority students in Mensa and for the program to be more inclusive. Of the 20 attendees at the event, there were only two African Americans in the room, me and the superintendent who was the host for the event. The others in the room were primarily white women. They were all against any encouragement to include minorities who did not meet the actual Mensa IQ requirement. However, their reasoning was because it would be more work for them to add students to their roster. None were interested in assisting minority students to be included in the process, or to assist in encouraging families to be included.

I spoke up, identifying myself as a parent. I'm sure many wondered why I was there; however, no one said anything to me. I told a story that a teacher told me in my youth, about two runners at the starting line of a race. One runner had trained all his life for the big race, with the best coaches, the best running shoes, the best food, and better hydration than his competitor. The second runner had shoes with holes in them, no coach, no food or water. Who do you think would win the race? The better prepared runner, of course.

My analogy fell flat with the teachers in the room, with the exception of the presenter and the superintendent. The teachers continued to complain about their workload. I was disappointed. The event only clarified for me that, as a parent, I would probably be the only person advocating for my children, and that I could not depend on teachers or anyone else to push for my children. I recommended to the host and speaker that they have a similar event for parents to attend, so they would know about the types of programs, like Mensa, that were available for their children. Mensa also has online programs for students regardless of IQ. They thought it was a good idea, but I never heard back from them.

I was happy I was in the room to get information I was not previously aware of. I passed the Mensa information on to several families to encourage them to see if their children were eligible for the organization. Readers, you may want to research whether Mensa may be an option for your children.

Always be aware of your children's strengths and challenges. If you see an area that your child is intimidated by, address it by encouraging them to take it on and tackle it. It will help them and build their confidence in the long run.

Extracurricular Activities

It's okay to have your child involved in sports. However, do not focus all their time on sports at the expense of their academic growth. Your child is unlikely to make a living at sports. They need to get a college degree or some type of training and get a job that will allow them to make a living and live on their own. I have taken my children and other children to see Dr. Ben Carson, the world-renowned neurosurgeon. He reminded the children in his presentation that they were unlikely to make a living at sports, and only a few won't end up financially broke after their sports careers are cut short due to injuries, or they lose their spot on the team.

I do believe that all able-bodied children should participate in a sport, whether it is dance, yoga, or – like my children – soccer, basketball, lacrosse, and volleyball. My children played an instrument as well – violin and piano.

Also, be sure to have your child involved in community service, working at homeless shelters, or playing with children with disabilities. I recommend volunteering with the Special Olympics, as my children did. Girl Scouts and Boy Scouts are also good programs.

Private schools, enrichment programs, colleges and great job opportunities look for students with well-rounded experiences in academics, sports, and community service. Teach your child to have a sense of duty. Life is not just about them.

Testing is a significant part of the education system. Many minority students do not do well in standard testing situations within their school setting. Some minority students don't do well in testing for higher level private high school with test like the SSAT or PSAT, or IESS for middle school, and SAT/ACT for college. Why is this?

I believe it is because our children are not being challenged in school, home, or in the community. In my opinion, to do well, a child has to have experiences, lots of exposure to reading, math, and positive, interesting people who have excelled. It is important to get them used to taking tests and learning to analyze. I believe this is because many do not prepare outside of the home or school. Many great students who test well do so because parents pay for private tutors. Consider paying $200 for a tutor and forgo the $200 pair of sneakers for your child. Help your child have a phenomenal, verifiable resume that will help sell their abilities when applying for any competitive program. See an example of my daughter's resume. My children have had resumes since elementary school. My youngest since she was 5 years old.

How I Became an Activist for My Children's Education

Photo
Name
Age/Grade:
Parents:
Home/Cell:
Emails:

Education:
School Name - 9th grade - Aug 2011- Present
- International Baccalaureate (IB) Higher Level Diploma Programme
- Duel Languages Mandarin and French
- Model UN, School Ambassador, Community Service, School Choir, Girl-Up School Club Founder

Academic Achievement/Honors:
- Authored and Illustrated Children's book about Inge Auerbacher, Holocaust Survivor - Aug 2013
- Congressional Award for Volunteer Service/Leadership from Congressman Gerry Connelly, (D-VA), featured in Washington Post - 2008
- Johns Hopkins Center for Talent Youth, 2006- Present
- National Honor Society – 2005-2010
- DOD Mathematics and Science program, George Washington University June 2009/2012
- A Better Chance Scholar – 2011 to present
- Studied Mandarin at Astar Education Institute, 2010
- Winner Regional Art contest sponsored by Marymount College, May 2010
- Letters from President and Mrs. Obama for community service and Congressional award
- Founding member and President, Future Leaders Youth Book Club, 2005-2012

Leadership:
- State Department Teen Flight Leader to Kazakhstan (former Soviet Union) – Jul 2013
- United Nation Foundation Girl Up 1st Annual Leadership Conference –Mar 2012
- Leadership Conference, UCLA, California – July 2011
- Toastmasters International Leadership, certificate, May 2010

Community Service:
- Hosted fundraiser and Gala, volunteer for the Election of President Obama and other elected officials - Oct 2008/2012
- Congressional Award event volunteer honoring Ms. Lee, CEO of BET, Jun 2012
- Tutored Mason Life student with disability in reading/math, featured in local newspaper 2008-2010
- Volunteer, polls during local and national elections - 2000 - Present
- Volunteer, homeless shelters, senior center, church and schools in the community – 2000 - present

Extracurricular activities:
- School
  - Community Service Club, Model UN Club, School Choir, Black Student Club
  - Cappella Salon Singing Club
- Play violin
- Play Piano

Sport Activities:
- High School Varsity Volleyball, Basketball Championship (2013) and Lacrosse
- Basketball Championship for Basketball and Track and Field Middle School, 2006-2010
- Gymnastic World Aerobic and Gymnastic team, and Dance 2008-2011

Danielle's resume

RESUME NOTE: This is just an example. You can use any one-page resume format you desire. The goal is to capture your child's accomplishments and modify the resume to include the relative information based on what they are applying for. It is a living document. You can also do a Brag sheet, paragraph or a short half page bio.

Sandra Manigault of the Manigault Institute, a tutoring and SAT/ACT prep company with 40 years of experience, tutored my children with her husband Donald. She says this about why minority students may not do well on SAT and other standardized tests:

> "I have realized basic differences in expected outcomes. That is, obviously students who can prep rigorously for the SAT will do better than those who cannot. Students who take AP English have a huge "leg up" on the essay and other English components. Students who are "A" math students and have taken the more rigorous math courses will do better without prepping. In other words, environment, opportunity, money, and drive, or some combination of these, matter a lot."

We need to help our children get into good schools and colleges. Better test scores usually mean larger financial aid packages and scholarship opportunities. Before you buy those $200+ sneakers or designer label jackets, use that money to get your child a great private tutor. You can also find another student to tutor your child in exchange for community service hours. These supports can help prepare them for high level tests and summer enrichment programs. Your child will be successful enough to get a great job and buy their own $200 sneakers.

My son, Darryl, has a learning disability. However, we pushed him to have a life like his sisters. He received the "Exceptional Child, Yes I Can" award for students with disabilities. He completed George Mason University's Mason Life program, and completed internships with several congressmen's offices on Capitol Hill. He also received the Congressional Gold Medal for over 1,000 hours of community service, personal development, and exploration.

When Darryl was 10 years old, I realized he liked working on the computer. One of his teachers told me about a summer program for students with disabilities at the Hellen Keller Institute at George Mason University, where they were conducting a pilot program for students with disabilities. I signed him up. He did well in the program, learning how to focus, retain information learned, and speech therapy.

My path to building my children's abilities started by reading to them and playing games like Monopoly, Scrabble and Trivial Pursuit and continued into more advanced programs. Wherever I go, I encourage parents to start where they are. Sometimes you have to be the one person in your friend group to get things started. I have served as a volunteer and application evaluator for a number of enrichment and scholarships programs. One great program is the Smithsonian Programs for Youth.

The Smithsonian offers fun and challenging (and sometimes mind-blowing) experiences for K-12 students interested in science, nature, technology, art, design, history, culture, or all of the above. These programs build confidence and skills of self-expression, communication, leadership, and provide college and career preparation, in extraordinary museum environments. My children participated in several of their programs, most of which were free. They have programs online as well.

My goal in volunteering was to understand the programs so I could advise my children on how to apply. Also, there was no conflict of interest with me evaluating these programs as long as I did not evaluate applications of students I knew or knew of. Otherwise, the student would be disqualified. In addition, the programs have many layers to the selection process across organizations, and some are fully funded by the Department of State, and no one person could ensure the selection of any individual. My children, and others that I advised, were selected for these very competitive programs based on their accomplishments, resumes, applications, and interviews.

CHAPTER THREE

THE RIGHT PATH

I started on this journey over twenty years ago to enhance my knowledge and understanding of enrichment opportunities for my children. In doing so, I've assisted over 200 families in acquiring approximately $10 million in scholarships for college, travel abroad programs and other enrichment programs to give students opportunities that typically only the well-to-do are able to experience. My children, and other students I've assisted, have attended private schools on scholarships at some of the best schools in the U.S. and participated in travel abroad trips to China, Spain, South Africa, Cuba, Kazakhstan, Turkey, and Kenya, just to name a few. Others were programs like the Johns Hopkins Center for Talented Youth, as well as law, STEM, entrepreneur, medical, and art programs for children. Many of my students and families would have never considered sending their children to a private boarding or day school. However, after seeing the success of my children, almost all of the families I counseled applied for—and most were accepted—at these prestigious private schools for middle and high school aged students.

I would host information sessions at my home and eventually the A Better Chance (ABC) organization started conducting official information sessions at the Sidwell Friends school (where the

Obama daughters attended). I personally recruited approximately 200 families in the District of Columbia, Maryland, and Virginia (DMV) area for ABC. The chapter became one of the most well-organized, and successful chapters in the national organization under the leadership of its Mid-Atlantic Region Program Manager, from 2000-2018.

A Better Chance is an organization that identifies, recruits and develops leaders among young people of color throughout the United States. Many of the students that apply are from disadvantaged families, and are selected for consideration to attend highly selective public, private, and charter schools throughout the U.S. My girls were privileged during their high school years to be selected as ABC scholars and were awarded scholarships.

Additionally, the ABC program was started in the 1960s by President Kennedy to ensure less represented groups of students had the opportunity to apply for and be selected to attend the best middle schools and high schools in the country. I first heard about ABC from a friend at my church when she told a group of us about her experience as an ABC scholar, 30 years prior, as a high school student. I decided, if I ever had children, I would have them participate in the A Better Chance process. One of my other friends was in the same group and she had a daughter as well. She decided to apply to ABC and was the first of my friend's children to attend an ABC affiliated school in Richmond, VA. Her daughter, Helene, was also both my girls' mentor growing up.

We attended several of Helene's events at her boarding school, and my oldest daughter decided she wanted to attend when she was older. The school became only a day school after ending their boarding program, so Marguerite was not able to attend as we lived two hours away. Instead, she attended another boarding school for girls in Maryland, also two hours from our home, on scholarship. We only had to pay her incidentals. She did exceptionally well. She was voted school president and May Queen during her senior year – the first African American girl to do so. My shy, introverted daughter was the school president and May Queen. I couldn't believe it. Marguerite was well-liked at her high school by her peers and faculty. She worked hard at her studies, participated in clubs and activities, played basketball and volleyball, sang in an a cappella group and did many hours of community service. She became a leader at the school.

When it was time for the school election of officers, Marguerite was supporting one of her friends who was planning to run. I asked her why she didn't run, and she said because her friend was running. I reminded her of her own accomplishments, then asked her if her friend could win, due to some issues she had at school. I told Marguerite she could win and told her to talk to her school advisor and her science teacher, to whom she and other girls frequently turned for advice. They both encouraged her to run for president. She did, and the rest is history. Her friend did not run in the end and was upset with Marguerite for a long time. However, they still keep in touch. Marguerite applied for and was selected for the ABC award, which was awarded at an annual event in NYC and included money for college.

I hosted many ABC information sessions at my home and my daughters' elementary school, Cardinal Montessori in Woodbridge, VA. I spoke at other sessions as a subject matter expert in boarding school applications, interviewed prospective students, and served as the Virginia representative and an ABC advisory board member. I also hosted events at my home for students and families who were accepted as ABC scholars and were going to private/public affiliated schools. I would invite my daughters and their friends, who were already in the program, to talk to the students in student-only sessions while I spoke to the parents. There were times when I would have 50 people in my home for these events.

Sending your children away to boarding school was not something that many Black families ever considered. It was very foreign to them. But I felt having a support network was important for families to be able to ask questions of someone who was actually attending boarding school or had attended. I would also have older college students who completed the program come back and share their personal stories. Marguerite was always delighted to tell her story and all of the students looked up to her, including her little sister. Helene, who mentored both my girls, would share her experience as well. In addition, most of the private boarding programs offered day school as well for local students, for families who were only interested in day schools.

One of the students I recommended applied to ABC, but was not accepted. Her mother and the student were devastated and the mom called me very upset. I told the mother I would look into the matter. I made a call, and the next day the student received an acceptance notice. She went on to be accepted into a great boarding school and did very well. Part of my work as an advocate and an activist is also going to bat on behalf of other parents and children who do not have the extensive experience that I do.

May 20, 2020

Mrs. Lyle, my mentor in high school, was an influential force in helping me not only apply to but get into the extremely selective State Department Travel Abroad Scholarship Program to Greece for a month when I was 17 years old. The scholarship was worth $25K. It was a lot of firsts for me: first time flying, traveling alone, and going off to another country entirely. It presented me with a once in a lifetime opportunity to go abroad and immerse myself into a culture much different from my own and challenged me in unique ways. If it were not for her guidance and determination, I would not have been so lucky. To this day, it is still an experience that I look back on fondly. I have been selected as a PhD candidate at Virginia Tech and other universities, and credit Mrs. Lyle for many of my successes to date.

Very Respectfully,

L. Currie

****

July 3, 2017

Dear Mrs. Lyle,

Thank you so much for referring me to Running Start! It was an amazing experience and I'm so glad I was a part of it. I also want to thank you for being my mentor.

- *M. Burnard**

*This student received a $1,500 scholarship to attend Running Start and went on to be awarded $1.4M in scholarships for college.

CHAPTER FOUR

IT STARTS AT HOME

Marguerite

When Marguerite was in the seventh grade, I made her sign up for the Martin Luther King (MLK) Oratorical contest sponsored by the local Delta Sigma Theta Sorority to represent her school. She was very shy and I wanted her to get out of her comfort zone. The contest was an annual Prince William County (PWC) contest featuring all the middle and high schools in the county. The event attracted both the TV and news media, like the *Washington Post*, and the winners of the contest would be featured.

Marguerite was tall and always wanted to be in the background, not noticed. She was 5'10 by the time she was thirteen years old, where the average height of her peers was 5'3, so she was teased a lot growing up. My goal was for her to embrace herself as God made her, and not to let others make her feel like she was less than anyone else because of her height. I told her the girls and boys who teased her were jealous because they wished they were tall. As a short person, I acted like I was tall and towered over folks with my outgoing personality and confidence. I wanted her as a tall person to act tall and confident.

There were five other students from her school competing for the same spot. Each student worked with the school coach and had to select a topic to write their speech about. Marguerite's speech was a letter to her peers about how to work toward greatness as they defined it, how to do well in school, and to be courteous to their peers and others as they prepared to be the future leaders of their community and country.

I told her I did not care if she won the contest, I just wanted her to have the experience of preparing for and presenting before people and getting comfortable with it, as it would help her later in life – in college and the professional world. She said, "If I have to do this, then I want to win!" That was all I needed to hear. I was going to give her the tools to prepare her to be a winner. She went into "full court press" preparation mode.

I contacted a deaconess at our church who was an elder and former English and drama teacher – as well as an oratory winner herself – to coach her in how to present her speech. After reading Marguerite's speech, however, she didn't agree with most of it as she though it may be too "racy." I explained that the speech was a message to her peers who would understand where she was coming from, and that the speech was not a message to old folks like us. Yes, she continued to try to get Marguerite to delete sentences.

Marguerite, who was taught to always be respectful of her elders, politely said she did not want to change the speech. Mrs. Harris finally relented, and she worked with Marguerite every day for two weeks after school on how to present her speech. After the two weeks of training, I brought Marguerite to friend's homes and invited others to our house so she could give her speech in front of them and receive criticism from loved ones. They were amazed that the tall, quiet, shy, twelve-year old, who rarely spoke above a whisper, could be heard throughout the house giving her speech in a confident, booming voice. She was ready.

At her school, each student had to give their speech during an all-school assembly. Several of the children stopped in the middle of their speeches and laughed out loud because children in the audience were deliberately trying to distract them. I moved to the front and took a seat to ensure she saw my, "You better not let your friends distract you," face. She worked harder than anyone else at her school, and the school selected her to represent them in the county-wide contest.

Later, Marguerite and 20 other middle school students went before the judges panel, made up of teachers, professors, elected officials, and others from the PWC community, representing their school in the hopes of being selected as one of three middle schoolers to present before an audience. She was one of the three selected in the middle school category.

Two days later, Marguerite was on stage in front of news cameras and an audience of 2,000 giving her speech. She was on fire. Her delivery was electrifying, and she worked the large stage talking to everyone in the crowd. One of my friends, who knew how shy Marguerite was, cried as she watched and listened to her. She repeatedly said, "I can't believe that is Marguerite!"

Marguerite won.

The same day, ABC, NBC and CBS local news featured her on TV. The next morning, the *Washington Post* featured her on the front page with a write-up and her photo.

After her win, she was asked by George Mason University to present her speech for a luncheon of professors and scholars, with featured TV commentator and author, Juan Williams. He congratulated her on her speech and win. In addition, George Mason University officials told her there would be admission and scholarships for her if she elected to attend college there after graduating high school. Marguerite went on to give her speech for government agencies, Black History Month celebrations, and also presented at several churches.

Marguerite is now a confident, but humble, young lady who knows that with preparation, she can take on and be successful with any challenge. This was her awakening. She has progressed over the years, taking on everything in a graceful way and with strength, knowing who she is. She found her voice.

In high school, she attended many programs that furthered her growth into a brilliant young woman with a passion for helping others. She attended one of the first Running Start, Young Women's

Leadership programs founded by its CEO, Susannah Wellford, as a freshman in high school with a scholarship. Running Start is a nonpartisan, nonprofit program that empowers young women to get involved in politics. They teach and inspire hands-on skills and confidence needed to run and win, so they can eventually transform our world, one elected female leader at a time. The program helps young women run for office, whether in high school, college, a local community or a national elected office.

For college, Marguerite was accepted at the University of Virginia, Amherst College, George Washington College, Georgetown University, and Case Western University. In the end, she wanted to move away to college, instead of staying in the Virginia-DC area. Wheaton College in Massachusetts offered her a full scholarship of approximately $200K for four years. Marguerite received $500K in total offers. She attended Wheaton College on academic scholarship for her undergraduate degree, and now lives and works in New York City while completing her master's degree.

A Better Chance award

It Starts at Home

Baccalaureate Ceremony
Class of 2010

Opening Music	Adagio for Organ – Frank Bridge
Processional	Trumpet Tune in D – Henry Purcell
Hymn #8 *"Morning Has Broken"* A Gaelic Melody	Congregation
Welcome	The Reverend Megan Stewart-Sicking
A Litany of Remembrance and Hope	The Senior Class
The First Reading, First Corinthians 13: 1-13	Marguerite Copeland School President
The Second Reading An Irish Blessing	Maddie Cole Senior Class President
Introduction of Baccalaureate Speaker	Taylor Smith, Head of School
Address	Anne and Jim Weeks
Closing Remarks	Taylor Smith, Head of School
School Song – *"The Sheep on the Hill"*	The Senior Class
Benediction	The Reverend Megan Stewart-Sicking
Recessional	Rondeau – Jean Joseph Mouret

MAGUERITE COPELAND
Member School: Oldfields College Preparatory School | Hometown: Woodbridge, VA

Marguerite is the school President of Oldfields College Preparatory School. In addition, she is actively involved in several organizations including Future Educators Association, Black Awareness Club (B.A.C.), Playmakers Theater Group, FOCUS and serves as co-captain of the Varsity Volleyball team. Marguerite takes her enthusiasm and dedication outside of school as well. Over the years, she has worked on six political campaigns, including the 2008 Presidential Campaign of President Barack Obama, mentored for the Future Leaders Youth Book Club in her community, and participated actively in her local church as part of the band and Junior Usher Board. In 2009, Marguerite traveled to Spain for four weeks as one of the summer Experiment in International Living Ambassadors. Marguerite will attend Wheaton College in the fall.

Marguerite, School President

Press Release Naomi Tutu

PRESS RELEASE

Growing up in apartheid South Africa, Nontombi Naomi Tutu saw injustice firsthand, but she also learned how dedicated activists can change the world for the better. And she has dedicated herself to doing so.

On September 16, Wheaton College will present the advocate for tolerance, equality, and human rights with the Otis Social Justice Award. The 7 p.m. presentation will take place in Hindle Auditorium in the Science Center, and Tutu will deliver a lecture titled "Striving for Justice: Searching for Common Ground."
Her father, Archbishop Desmond Tutu, won the Nobel Peace Prize for his role in ending the apartheid regime. She has had a wide range of experiences, serving as a development coordinator in West Africa, founding a consulting firm, leading reconciliation efforts for feuding groups, and teaching at several American universities.

Nontombi Naomi Tutu's selection for the award was first proposed by Marguerite Copeland '14, who is majoring in African, African American Diaspora Studies.
Marguerite's family hosted an event for Girl Up, United Nations Foundation, a program that supports American girls who raise awareness and funds for girls in developing countries. At the event, Tutu spoke about the importance of young women becoming leaders in their community. Marguerite said she was inspired by Tutu's speech and by the stories of the young girls who are involved in Girl Up. Afterward, Marguerite worked with the Dean of Students, Lee Williams and Professor of Women's Studies, Kim Miller, who has researched women activists in South Africa, to have Tutu speak at Wheaton.

The Otis Social Justice lecture series was established in 1959 through the generosity of Henry Witte Otis, whose children included two Wheaton graduates. Eleanor Roosevelt was among the earliest Otis lecturers (1962). The first Otis Social Justice Award was presented in 1990 to former U.S. Surgeon General C. Everett Koop. Today, Otis Fund supports a colloquium in social justice—a forum through which the Wheaton community may address key contemporary social issues.

This year's lecture will celebrate Wheaton's new minor, Peace and Social Justice Studies. The minor is an interdisciplinary study of injustice, activism, and community organizing. Professor Miller, who will be teaching some of the courses in the minor, said that Tutu's selection for the Otis award and lecture highlights the fact that Wheaton is a community that cares about issues of social justice and equality.

Darryl

Darryl is the oldest of my three children. He has a Developmental Disability (DD). However, we did not let that stop him from having his successes as well.

Darryl was the first of my children to receive the Congressional Gold Medal for Youth and was the first child with disabilities ever to receive the Gold Medal. This award is a national award acknowledging great volunteer and personal development, as well as athletic achievement by young people around the country given by the Congressional Foundation for the U.S. Congress. Darryl completed his requirements for the Gold Medal over a two-year period, the least amount of time to complete the requirements. He volunteered at the Library of Congress, political campaigns, nursing homes and homeless shelters. He attended and was selected to be a guest speaker at several conferences for students and parents of children with disabilities.

After his presentation at the Annual Disability Education and Transition Conference as an associate in Richmond, VA, the father of a baby with a disability came up to Darryl and told him he'd given the father hope that his young son would grow up to be actively involved and successful in the community in spite of his disability. In addition, Darryl was awarded the "Yes I Can" national award for people with disabilities who have overcome adversity in spite of their disabilities. My husband took Darryl to the ceremony in Nashville, TN to get his award. It was a proud day for Darryl and our family.

Darryl, in spite of his disability received scholarships to attend the George Mason University, Mason Life Program.

Darryl received the Council for Exceptional Children "Yes I Can" Award in Nashville TN for students with disabilities.

"Yes I Can" award

Darryl had an opportunity to attend and graduate from George Mason University's (GMU) Mason Life program. The program allows college age students to receive a college experience at the academic level they need. He received $80K in scholarships to attend the Mason Life program at GMU. Darryl volunteered at the Library of Congress (LOC), where a good friend who works there recommended him, and became his job mentor. After two years of volunteer work and one paid summer internship, the LOC hired him full-time with full pay and benefits. He has now just completed six years at the LOC and is going strong. Not bad for a young man who had a teacher in the Philadelphia school system once say he would not be able to function in the real world and could only hope to get a job cleaning toilets, land in jail, or die young. I guess he showed her!

Darryl had a wonderful special education middle school teacher, Mrs. Graham, who always looked out for him, and shared information about opportunities in the county for students with disabilities. Her son and niece both had disabilities, so she was familiar with available programs. She told me about the Virginia Postsecondary Education Rehabilitation Transition (PERT) Program. She encouraged me to apply for Darryl to participate when he got to high school, although her son and niece did not meet the requirement to attend.

The PERT Program is a highly effective, school-to-work transition initiative supported by the Virginia Department of Education and administered through the Virginia Department of Aging and Rehabilitative Services (DARS) at Wilson Workforce and Rehabilitation Center (WWRC). I applied for the PERT Program for Darryl when he turned sixteen years old. I took him to the campus so we could do a tour and determine if he wanted to attend if selected. He was excited to go away for 2 weeks in the summer to a place set up like a college campus. After I submitted Darryl's application, I was told he was approved for PERT. The whole family was excited for this opportunity for Darryl. PERT is a very competitive program that only accepts 20 students statewide per year. I knew Darryl had a great chance of getting a slot.

A few weeks after I was told Darryl would get the next PERT slot for our county, I met a parent whose son transferred into the school from out of state and was new to Darryl's class. The mom and I hit it off immediately. We talked about the challenges of being a parent of a child with disabilities, and how everything was extra difficult when dealing with the school system, IEP's, etc. On one occasion she saw me and was excited to say that the teacher told her about a new program that she had never heard of, and that her son was selected to go to the PERT program from the class. I held my composure and expressed how happy I was for her son.

After we finished our conversation, I immediately went to see the teacher, asking why my son did not get the slot for PERT as promised, and why instead his slot was given to a new student who had just transferred in. The teacher said she was sorry, but the paperwork was already processed for the other student, and it would not be fair to cancel him, and put Darryl in the slot. I paused then asked why it was fair to give Darryl's slot away, and not keep her word to him and our family. I was upset by her cavalier attention concerning my son. Further, I felt she was discriminating against Darryl as a black student due to the fact the new student was white. She said Darryl would have to wait until next year.

I left her class and went to the Principal's office and scheduled an appointment for the next day. I had also requested the Assistant Principal for Special Education attend as he was familiar with PERT and knew Darryl was next in line to attend. During the meeting, I asked that Darryl be given a slot and I informed them I would not take no for an answer. I expressed that I felt the decision was discriminatory against Darryl and reminded them that they gave away Darryl's promised slot to the other student who happened to be white. They asked how I knew the other student was selected, so I told them to check their records. I also informed them I would be making an appointment with the county school superintendent and my congressman if necessary, if Darryl did not have a slot. Two days later, Darryl came home with a letter congratulating him on his selection for PERT. He was so excited. The other student and Darryl were both going to PERT.

I did not hold any animosity with the parent, she had no idea that Darryl was slated for PERT. She was told by the teacher to apply and ensured that she would get her son a slot. However, I did write a letter to the teacher and school principals thanking them for ensuring Darryl got a slot, and spoke privately with the teacher about how disappointed I was in her. After that, the same teacher became Darryl's biggest champion for the next two years until his graduation from high school.

After high school, Darryl went to work at Didlake*. Didlake is an internationally accredited nonprofit agency providing Employment and Day Support Services. Their rehabilitative services are customized to meet the unique needs of each individual and they collaborate with community members and local businesses to find competitive employment and hire people with disabilities. Didlake finds that

---

* https://www.didlake.org/

people, regardless of their abilities, tend to perform to the level of expectation that is set for them. They begin with high expectations for every person and when those expectations are met, they set the bar even higher.

Darryl got a job at the Pentagon working as a custodian through Didlake. After one year there, I applied for Darryl to attend George Mason University's Mason Life Program. The Mason Life Learning into Future Environments (LIFE) Program is a supportive academic university experience that offers a four-year postsecondary curriculum of study to students with intellectual and developmental disabilities (IDD) who begin the program between 18-23 years of age. Mason Life was the first of its kind in the country and has been used as a model for other university's programs for people with disabilities around the country.

The program had a very competitive selection process. Darryl and I were both interviewed for admission to Mason Life. Darryl was selected, and the program cost $22K each year for 4 years. The program did not offer scholarships, nor did it qualify for Pell grants or any federal programs. I reached out to a parent who helped start the Mason Life program at GMU and found out that another parent, one of four parents who were instrumental in getting Mason Life approved, was the Chairman of a charity organization that provided scholarships for Mason Life students. The charity organization gave Darryl a scholarship each year to cover some of the cost. In addition, I reached out to Didlake and informed them that Darryl was selected for Mason Life. They were delighted to hear this because no other young adult who worked with him had been selected. I asked if they could provide a scholarship for Darryl. They informed me they had a foundation and provided me with an application. They paid for his four-year program at Mason Life.

At the time Darryl was with the Mason Life program, they did not provide housing. For the first year, I scheduled transportation to take Darryl back and forth to school while I worked. For the second year, a parent rented an apartment near the university and asked if Darryl and another student were interested in living in the apartment with their son while the parent and sister would be staying with them each night and driving them to classes each day. The boys would come home on the weekend. Darryl jumped at the chance to live away from home for college like his younger sister did. For his third and fourth years, the same parent rented a townhouse across from the University so the guys would be able to walk to classes each day. Each of the parents took turns staying over at the house to provide oversight in the house and to prepare meals or help the boys cook meals. Each parent was responsible for buying food for their child. Our arrangement worked well because each family was committed to making the process work.

During the summer months, Darryl volunteered at the Library of Congress (LOC). For his last year at Mason Life, I organized a schedule for Darryl to work four days a week volunteering at LOC and attend class only on Friday. LOC was happy to have the free labor, and Mason Life wanted to help Darryl get a full-time, paid position at LOC. It would be a feather in the programs cap if one of their students were hired into a federal job. It worked. Darryl has been a full time, paid, federal employee at the Library of Congress for six years. LOC has a very robust program to hire and retain people with disabilities. The staff there has been outstanding in helping and ensuring Darryl is successful at work.

Graduation Mason Life - Darryl

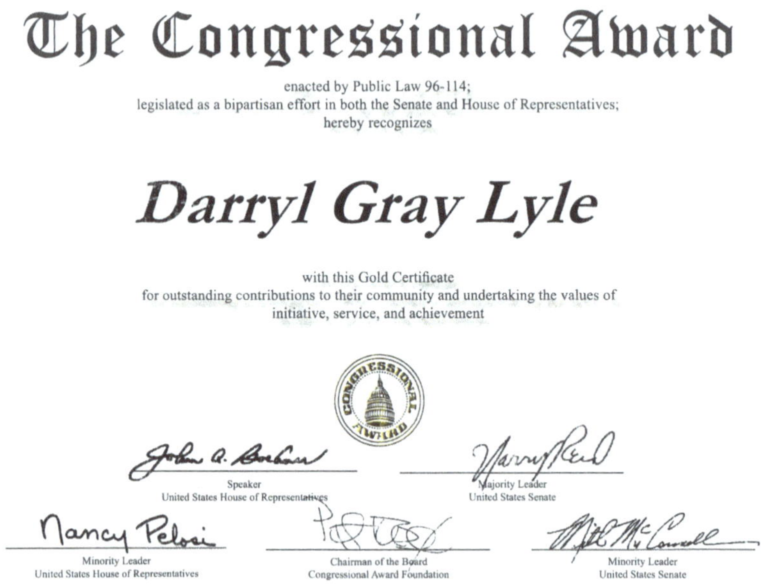

Rhonda Copeland Lyle

The Congressional Award

enacted by Public Law 96-114;
legislated as a bipartisan effort in both the Senate and House of Representatives;
hereby recognizes

Darryl Gray Lyle

with this Gold Certificate
for outstanding contributions to their community and undertaking the values of
initiative, service, and achievement

_____
John A. Boehner
Speaker
United States House of Representatives

_____
Harry Reid
Majority Leader
United States Senate

_____
Nancy Pelosi
Minority Leader
United States House of Representatives

_____
Chairman of the Board
Congressional Award Foundation

_____
Mitch McConnell
Minority Leader
United States Senate

Receiving Congressional Gold Medal on Capitol Hill, Washington DC with Senator and Chairman

Darryl receiving his Congressional Gold Medal from the U.S. Senator and the Chairman of the Congressional Youth Awards

Group photo with Darryl and other Congressional Gold Medal recipients on the steps of the Capitol Building in Washington, DC.

Rhonda Copeland Lyle

Library of Congress
101 Independence Ave., SE
Washington, DC 20540-2200

Human Resources Services
Office of Worklife Services
Customer Services Center

August 8, 2013

Dear Mr. Darryl E. Gray,

Congratulations on being selected for the position Support Clerk, (Receipt Analysis and Control Division, U.S. Copyright Office), Library of Congress. You will be paid as a GS-0303-02/01 at the annually rate of $24,865.00 (which includes locality pay).

You are scheduled to report for New Employee Orientation (NEO) and Entrance on Duty In-Processing on Monday, August 12, 2013 at 8:30 AM. Please report to the Human Resources Center at the Library of Congress, 101 Independence Ave, SE, Washington DC. (Note: You will be allowed entry into the building beginning at 8:30 AM.)

Please view the Human Resources Services Entry On Duty web site. On this web site you will find the administrative forms you must complete prior to taking the Oath of Office as an employee of the United States Government and reporting for work. Failure to complete forms and bring them on your first day may significantly delay your in processing.

Additionally, information on this website will familiarize you with the different types of benefits you are now eligible to receive as a government employee including health and life insurance, retirement and retirement savings plans. Your first day will be spent receiving an orientation to the Library of Congress. The Orientation Day program will end at 4:00 P.M. Please plan to stay until the program has concluded. When you report to the Library on your second day, you should report directly to your supervisor.

Vehicle parking in the vicinity of the James Madison Memorial Building is limited and parking is difficult. Many employees use Metrorail's Orange and Blue Line to the Capitol South station, as it is diagonally across the street from the James Madison Building.

We look forward to your joining the staff of the Library of Congress.

Sincerely,

A. Patterson
Human Resources Assistant

Library of Congress job award letter

It Starts at Home

The Congressional Award

Public Law 96-114, The Congressional Award Act

Board Officers
Chairman
PAXTON K. BAKER
BET Networks
Vice Chairwoman
DR. LINDA MITCHELL
MSU Extension Service
Vice Chairman
AMBASSADOR ROGER NORIEGA
Vision Americas LLC
Vice Chairman
HON. RODNEY E. SLATER
Patton Boggs, LLP
Secretary
MARY RODGERS
Pennsylvania
Treasurer
LEE KLUMPR CPA
BDO Seidman, LLP
Chairman Emeritus
JOHN M. FALK, ESQ.
Pinecrest Ltd.

Board Members
CLIFF AKIYAMA
Philadelphia College of Osteopathic Medicine
HON. MAX BAUCUS
U.S. Senator
HON. GUS BILIRAKIS
U.S. Representative
ED BLANSITT, CPA
Washington, DC
HON. KWAME R. BROWN
D.C. Council
LAUREL CALL
Ohio
NICK CANNON
California
MICHAEL CAROZZA
Briard-Myers Squibb
EDWARD L. COHEN
Lerner Enterprises
KATHY DIDAWICK
BlueCross BlueShield Association
DR. WILEY DOBBS
Idaho
MIKE ESSER
Edward Jones Investments
DAVID FALK
F.A.M.E.
MICHAEL FLANNIGAN
Peabody Energy
JEFFREY S. FRIED, ESQ.
Washington, DC
RON GILLIARD
California
GEORGE B. GOULD
Washington, DC
DR. LARRY GREEN
Maryland
J. STEVEN HART, ESQ
Williams & Jensen, P.C.
ERICA WHEELAN HEYSE *
National Director
DAVID W. HUNT, ESQ. *
Legal Counsel
HON. JOHNNY ISAKSON
U.S. Senator
HON. SHEILA JACKSON LEE
U.S. Representative
PAUL KELLY
National Association of Chain Drug Stores
ANNETTE LANTOS
California
CONRAD LASS
American Petroleum Institute
LYNN LYONS
Florida
PATRICK MCLAIN
small-aircraft, US
MARC MONYEK
McDonald's Corporation
PATRICK M. MURPHY
S Click Solutions
MAJOR GENERAL ROBERT B. NEWMAN, JR.
Virginia
KIMBERLY NORMAN
Texas
ANDREW R ORTIZ
Ortiz Leadership Systems
JERRY PROUT
FMC Corporation
GLENN REYNOLDS
US Telecom Association
ADAM RUIZ
Kentucky
DANIEL B. SCHERDER
Schenker & Associates
JIMMIE LEE SOLOMON
Major League Baseball
JEFFREY L. THOMPSON
The Walt Disney Company
HON. JERI THOMSON
Former Secretary, U.S. Senate
JOE WATSON
Virginia
KATHRYN WEEDEN
U.S. Senate Page School
JON WOOD
Alpha Natural Resources

* Ex Officio

12/27/2011

Darryl Gray

Dear Darryl:

On behalf of The Congressional Award National Board of Directors, I am pleased to inform you that you have earned the Congressional Award Bronze and Silver Medals. Along with these Medals, you have also qualified for the Congressional Award Bronze, Silver and Gold Certificates. We commend your willingness to give of yourself to voluntarily help others in the community and your achievements in personal development, physical fitness, and expedition.

Your accomplishments will be recognized with the presentation of the Silver Congressional Award Medal. You will be contacted regarding the details of this event. Please be patient, as it may take several months to arrange a presentation. Your Certificates and Bronze Medal are enclosed.

While you are waiting for your Silver Medal Ceremony, start working toward your Gold Medal. Work with your Advisor to establish new goals or to plan new activities if you are still pursuing your initial goals. You can begin as soon as your Advisor certifies that your goals and activities are personally challenging and meet the program guidelines.

Congratulations for successfully completing the requirements to earn the Congressional Award Bronze and Silver Medals. We are very proud of all you have accomplished!

Sincerely,

Paxton K. Baker
National Board of Directors
Chairman

379 Ford House Office Building • Washington, DC 20515 • (202) 226-0130 • FAX: (202) 226-0131
www.congressionalaward.org

Congressional silver award letter

Rhonda Copeland Lyle

PRINCE WILLIAM COUNTY'S ONLY LOCAL DAILY NEWSPAPER

Potomac News

Cuts to aid worry family

Proposed budget reduces funding for county programs

By KEITH WALKER
kwalker@potomacnews.com

Using flash cards, Darryl Gray, left, 18, practices his spelling and number recognition with the help cousin Danielle Lyle, 9, and his aunt Rhonda Lyle in their Woodbridge residence on Friday.

Darryl Gray is an affable guy who is always has a ready smile.

The 18-year-old says he's good at "fixing stuff and putting things in order."

But he can't read and he'll need financial help to find a job when he graduates from the Community Based Instruction Program at Potomac High School.

The aid may not be there because of county budget cuts.

The Community Services Board, through its Mental Retardation Sheltered Employment Services program, pays organizations such as Didlake, the Association for Retarded Citizens and ServiceSource to place retarded clients in suitable jobs.

Gray's aunt, Rhonda Lyle, and her husband, Lionel, have cared for Gray since he was 10. Rhonda Lyle considers Gray her son.

She's worried that Gray won't be able to enter the work force and lead a productive life without the financial aid.

"The plan was that he would graduate on time with his peers because he has to feel that sense of accomplishment of having completed something and he's ready to transition to the next phase of his life," Rhonda Lyle said.

Gray, who often helps his 9-year-old cousin, Danielle Lyle, clean her room, is anxious to start that new phase, said Rhonda Lyle, who lives with her family in the River Falls on the Occoquan near the Old Hickory Golf Club.

"Darryl looks at himself as any other high school senior who's ready to move out into the world," said Rhonda Lyle, a logistics analyst for a government contractor.

"We want that for him. We want him to have a sense of independence," she said.

Danielle admits that Gray does a better job than she can at room cleaning.

In return, Danielle helps Gray with the lessons that he'll forget without daily practice.

Gray can write words such as cake, top, bee, bear and fish with the aid of the flash cards Danielle wield

"I know he needs help and that it's right to help him," D said.

Gray, who is teaching Dan ride a bike, has held down IKEA, Old Country Buffet, Bes ern, Panera Bread and the I with help from the program high school.

"Because he's so high funct he's been very successful in th munity based instruction throu school where he's going out and ing," Rhonda Lyle said. "He truly a success story."

See GRAY, P.

Potomac Newspaper picture with Darryl, Danielle and Rhonda

Danielle

The older children were the test case for me. I knew nothing about dealing with schools and programs for students with disabilities. As most families know, we learn on the fly. By the time my youngest was old enough for me to start looking for opportunities for her, I was a veteran. My youngest daughter received her Congressional Gold Medal for Youth on Capitol Hill in 2016. This national award is given to students ages of 13.5 - 24 years old who have set and met goals in the areas of community service, personal development, athletics, and exploration over a two-year period. There is a gala and award program for the students in Washington, DC over a two-day period featuring the Congressperson, Senators, industry CEOs and celebrities from around the country. Danielle got a chance to meet Senator Mark Warner of Virginia and take a photo with him and other students from Virginia. Her actual gold medal was presented to her by Congresswoman Sheila Jackson Lee of Texas, because none of the Virginia Congresspersons or Senators were available.

At the age of twelve, Danielle was selected to attend the Leadership Academy, sponsored by Dr. Cornel West and Tavis Smiley at UCLA in California for one week. The cost was $400, plus the cost of her plane ticket. I asked if they offered scholarships and was told no because the academy cost was already being offset by several sponsors. I sent them a copy of Danielle's resume and they reconsidered, giving her a $400 scholarship to participate. We only paid the $400 for her round trip to California and return to Virginia. Now, could we afford to pay the $400 for the academy? Yes, but why not ask? Danielle traveled to California with a fellow book club child and long-time friend, Marcus. I helped him get into the program as well. After her experience in California, she said she wanted to attend UCLA. She met other young children from all over the country and loved meeting Dr. Cornel West, though she had previously seen him preach at Howard University in the Rankin Chapel in Washington, DC.

Danielle also had an opportunity to attend a Girl Leadership program with girls from around the world for two weeks in the summer when she was fourteen. The purpose of the program is to inspire high school girls ages 14-16 in "leadership with workshops, field trips to the United Nations in NYC, visiting career sites in NYC hosted by accomplished female leaders and gaining a global perspective on leadership and diplomacy." The workshops were held at Vassar College in New York.

Danielle completed a very extensive application with several essays required. She was one of the 20 girls selected out of approximately 150 girls who applied. She was excited to be selected and have a chance to visit NYC without her mom. The challenge for me was the cost: $2,500 for two weeks, plus airfare. Scholarships were offered, however, we did not qualify due to our income level. I did what I do best. I had Danielle send me a copy of her resume. She was away at her first year of boarding school and did not have time to follow-up with her application after she submitted it. I sent the program her resume and asked if they could waive the tuition cost and give her a scholarship.

They were so impressed with her resume and a voice message she left about how much she wanted to attend. We only had to pay the non-refundable deposit of $200 and her airplane ticket. She also found out another student from the northern Virginia area was also attending the leadership program and they coordinated getting the same flight so they could travel together. I took her to the airport, put her on the plane for two weeks of fun, meeting new girls from around the world, and learning from the movers and shakers of the world. She had a great time and came back ready to take on anything.

For parents who are concerned about coming up with money, don't despair. Consider setting up a GoFundMe page, ask your employer if they will sponsor your child to participate in worthwhile programs, and/or ask your church for assistance. Be sure to provide proof that the money raised was used for the intended purpose. Also, have your child write thank you cards. They can send thank you emails, but also have them take the time and effort to send an actual thank you card. Folks will remember and appreciate it. You

It Starts at Home

never know when you may need to reach out again for help, and it teaches the child to be appreciative to others who helped them.

Danielle's accomplishments continued in the area of writing. Danielle wrote and illustrated her first children's book when she was fourteen years old. This opportunity came about while I was at a conference in Washington, DC for a foreign exchange program I volunteered with. I met a woman from Iowa who told me she was a publisher with her own company, and was looking for middle school and high school students to write children's books about living survivors of the Holocaust. She indicated that there was a Holocaust survivor who lived in NYC named Inge Auerbacher, who had contacted her about her writing project, and wanted a young person to write her story about surviving a concentration camp from the age of seven to ten years old.

The publishers had only worked with students and families in Iowa though she asked me if I knew a young person who might want to write Inge's story. Well, of course, I volunteered my daughter. I texted her at school and asked if she wanted to do the book over the summer since she liked to write and draw. She immediately replied with, "Of course I'll write Inge's story, because I know you already told the lady I would." It was true, I had. Over the summer, in between my daughter going to the beach and hanging out with friends, she read the first book Inge published about her life in Germany and the concentration camp, "I Am a Star, Child of the Holocaust". She then called to interview her over the phone. The book Danielle wrote and illustrated was about Inge surviving a concentration camp with her doll. That doll is at the U.S. Holocaust Memorial Museum in Washington, DC.

I invited Inge to come to Virginia to view Danielle's work and help select the drawings she had completed. Inge was surprised to get such an invitation but was happy to accept. She arrived at Union Station in DC and called me. I knew what she looked like from her Facebook page, but she had no idea what I looked like. At the time I did not have any photos on my Facebook page. When I walked up to her and introduced myself, she shouted out, "You are Black, what a special surprise! This is perfect. A young African American child writing my story – an old Jewish lady. I love it!" She gave me a big hug and off we went to my home.

She stayed with us for two nights and was thrilled to be in our home and being involved in proofreading Danielle's book and the drawing selections. The book was published and is sold on Amazon. I also contacted the *Washington Post* about the book. They requested to do an interview with Danielle and Inge at the National Holocaust Museum in Washington, DC. The article was done and featured on the front page of the Post's local section. Soon after, the National Holocaust Museum contacted me again to ask if Danielle would be interested in doing a television commercial for the museum. Of course, we said yes. The commercial was aired on CNN during the Voices of Auschwitz 70th Anniversary Special hosted by Wolf Blitzer and sponsored by Academy Award director/producer Steven Spielberg. The commercial was also aired on the History, Military, and the American Heroes channels. Danielle was sixteen years old at the time of the commercial. She was asked to speak at schools and social events for children and was interviewed by another local newspaper.

In addition, Inge was presented with a special award by the German Ambassador at his private residence on Park Avenue in NYC after he saw the Washington Post article. Inge invited Danielle and I to attend.

Danielle is an adult now, and we still keep in touch with Inge who continues to travel the world speaking about the Holocaust through love and peace to ensure it, or anything like it, never happens again. Danielle was accepted at 10 colleges, many with scholarships, totaling approximately $300K. She elected to attend a Historically Black College/University (HBCU), Spelman College in Atlanta, Georgia.

The Washington Post

A bond that transcends age

Woodbridge teenager and Holocaust survivor form friendship over writing of book

BY JULIE ZAUZMER

Sixty-nine years after she was liberated from the Terezín concentration camp, Inge Auerbacher still gets choked up when she looks at the doll that she carried with her through her three horrible years in the Nazi camp.

This past weekend, the person who gently put an arm around her and rubbed her back while Auerbacher tearfully kissed that doll was an unlikely friend — Danielle Lyle, a 16-year-old from Woodbridge, Va.

Assigned to write about Auerbacher's experience a year ago, Lyle struck up a remarkably close friendship with the Holocaust survivor. Despite the gulf in their ages, races, religions and experiences, each said she considers the other one to be "like a sister."

"The Holocaust is taught about in school, it's not taught in a way that makes people listen to it and grasp what actually happened," said Lyle, who just finished her junior year at St. Timothy's School, an all-girls boarding school in Stevenson, Md. Now that she has heard Auerbacher's story, she said, "It hits you more."

The program "A Book by Me" started the connection between Lyle and Auerbacher. The initiative connects schoolchildren to Holocaust survivors, World War II veterans and others who are among the few remaining living witnesses to historic events. Each child interviews one of these subjects, then writes and illustrates a picture book to teach other children these elders' stories.

When Lyle was assigned to write the book, Auerbacher, 79, enjoyed their first phone call so much that she invited the teenager to visit her at her home in New York. Lyle's mother suggested that Auerbacher come to Woodbridge to stay as a guest in their home instead — so Auerbacher boarded a bus to meet the high school student and her family.

Auerbacher's story has been told all over the world — she has written six books, including a 1986 memoir, "I Am a Star: Child of the Holocaust," which has been translated into at least eight languages and is widely used as a teaching tool for lessons on the Holocaust. But Lyle thought she could tell it in a new way, and after spending time with Auerbacher, she felt compelled to do so.

Danielle Lyle looks on as Inge Auerbacher puts a homemade cap on her beloved doll. Auerbacher donated the doll to the U.S. Holocaust Memorial Museum in 1992.

". . . I feel like it's really important for her to tell her story. And any way I can help with that, I wanted to."

Danielle Lyle, on her collaboration with Inge Auerbacher

and World War II series created by "A Book by Me" and one of just eight chosen

against the racially and religiously insensitive comments she has heard in her own community.

"I'm black. And I'm not just black, I'm dark-skinned. And I'm a girl, going to a majority non-black school," she said. "I feel like it's still very relevant now."

Auerbacher agreed. Before she got off the bus from New York and saw Lyle's mother waiting for her, "I had no clue who they are, whether they're white, black, green, yellow, whatever. . . . I was really thrilled when I met her mom that they were African American. Perfect, I said. Perfect."

In the concentration camp, an adult

Danielle and I with Inge Auerbacher, the German Ambassador and his wife in NYC at the ambassador's private residence on Park Ave.

Washington Post article
June 9, 2014

It Starts at Home

Inge Auerbacher holds the doll that she carried as a child while being held captive in a Nazi concentration camp, as Danielle Lyle, a Woodbridge, VA, teenager assigned to write a book on Auerbacher looks on. (Julie Zauzmer/The Washington Post) https://www.washingtonpost.com/local/virginia-teenager-holocaust-survivor-form-friendship-over-writing-of-book/2014/06/09/cc9287aa-ef53-11e3-9ebc-2ee6f81ed217_story.html

Danielle and 4 of her book club friends meeting U.S. Supreme Court Associate Justice, the Honorable Sonia Sotomayor. Each student including my daughter went on to receive scholarships for academic enrichment programs, travel aboard and college over the years.

Some of the Future Leaders Book Club members meeting Supreme Court Justice Sotomayor

Rhonda Copeland Lyle

U.S. DEPARTMENT OF LABOR

HILDA L. SOLIS
U.S. SECRETARY OF LABOR

AND

SARA MANZANO-DÍAZ
WOMEN'S BUREAU DIRECTOR

WOMEN'S HISTORY MONTH

A CONVERSATION WITH

HONORABLE SONIA SOTOMAYOR
U.S. SUPREME COURT ASSOCIATE JUSTICE

2011 WOMEN'S HISTORY MONTH OBSERVANCE

THURSDAY, MARCH 17, 2011

U.S. DEPARTMENT OF LABOR
FRANCES PERKINS BUILDING
AUDITORIUM
200 CONSTITUTION AVENUE NW
WASHINGTON, DC 20210

WOMEN'S BUREAU
90 YEARS: STILL WORKING

US DOL Women's History Month – Sotomayor invite

Danielle as a 5th grader received a Congressional Records Award from Congressman Gerry Connolly of Northern Virginia for community service.

Congressional Record

Proceedings and Debates of the 111th Congress, First Session

WASHINGTON, D.C.

House of Representatives

Statement by Representative Gerald E. Connolly
Recognizing Danielle Marguerite Lyle

HON. GERALD E. CONNOLLY
OF VIRGINIA

MR. CONNOLLY: Madam Speaker, I rise today to recognize Danielle Marguerite Lyle for her leadership and commitment to the community that she has displayed in Prince William County.

Since the age of 5, Danielle has been involved in community activities. She has spent hundreds of hours volunteering with local organizations and other community activities. Since then, she has volunteered with numerous organizations such as the Hilda Barg Homeless Shelter, the Arc of Prince William County, senior homes, her local church and other programs. When asked, she says that she loves helping people and the community.

Danielle also knows how to take initiative and lead. She participated in the Junior National Young Leaders Conference (Jr NYLC) in April 2009, and served as President of the Future Leaders Children's Book Club. Danielle has also been recognized for her leadership and intellectual abilities through the Johns Hopkins Center for Talented Youth Program, George Mason University Young Writers summer and weekend workshop, and the University of Virginia Summer Enrichment Program.

Along with Danielle's volunteer and leadership accomplishments, she has also received many accolades. These include many semesters on her school's honor roll and winning the Martin Luther King Jr. writing contest for the 5th grade.

With all of this, she still finds time to play the violin and piano, be a member of the Creative and Performing Arts Center and participate in track and field, basketball and gymnastics.

Danielle's accomplishments would be noteworthy for any person. When her current age of 11 is factored in, these accomplishments are nothing short of remarkable.

Madam Speaker, I ask that my colleagues join me in recognizing this bright young student and applauding her commitment to volunteerism and leadership. Our communities benefit greatly from the action and dedication of citizens like Danielle.

Congressional Record statement recognizing Danielle

It Starts at Home

United States Department of State

Bureau of Educational and Cultural Affairs

Washington, DC 20522

www.state.gov

May 12, 2014

Dear Danielle Lyle:

On behalf of the U.S. Department of State, congratulations on being awarded a 2014 National Security Language Initiative for Youth (NSLI-Y) scholarship. This year, over 3,600 outstanding young Americans from across the United States applied to the NSLI-Y program, making the application process extremely competitive. Your selection as a NSLI-Y scholar is a wonderful achievement of which you and your family can be very proud.

As you know, NSLI-Y's primary focus is language acquisition. It is the first U.S. Department of State program to provide scholarships for high school age Americans to study language while living and engaging with people in Arabic, Chinese, Hindi, Korean, Persian, Russian, and Turkish-speaking countries. I encourage you to think of your Chinese studies as a stepping stone to future language programs, as well as to the lifelong learning and use of foreign languages in both your academic and professional careers. At the conclusion of your program, you will be part of an exciting alumni network of more than one million students and professionals from around the world who have participated in U.S. government-sponsored exchange programs, including over 3,000 NSLI-Y alumni.

NSLI-Y scholars play an important role in representing the United States as citizen ambassadors – a responsibility we hope you take seriously as you meet and interact with people overseas. Indeed, as you are immersed in the culture and language of China, you will have many opportunities to share your thoughts and experiences about what it means to be an American and a global citizen – and you will learn to do it in Chinese! You will also experience firsthand the power of language to create bonds of friendship, respect, and understanding across cultures. In doing so, you will be helping to create a more peaceful future for all of us.

Again, congratulations on your acceptance into the NSLI-Y program, and for having the enthusiasm, curiosity, and desire to learn the language of another culture. Please also extend my appreciation to your parents or guardians for supporting you in this important endeavor. I wish you a rewarding summer of language study in China, and a lifetime of engaging with the world.

Sincerely,

Michele Peters
Branch Chief, Youth Programs Division
Office of Citizen Exchanges

Danielle Dept of State NSLI-Y award letter

Rhonda Copeland Lyle

Potomac News article with African Princess

Danielle Lyle

With

Princess Ncengencenge (Nancy) Dlamini of Swaziland Western Africa.

Danielle and her Book club members made a special presentation (written by Danielle) to the Princess giving her money they raised and books for the children orphaned by AIDS in Swaziland.

July 2007

My children and I: Darryl 16, Danielle 7, and Marguerite 13

My adult children as of 2020: Darryl 28, Marguerite 25 and Danielle 19

CHAPTER FIVE

WHEN YOUNG PEOPLE TAKE THE LEAD

Helene, the daughter of my friend Angela, who was about twelve, at the time, was a mentor and support for my two girls. Helene was my oldest daughter's math tutor when she was in third grade. She would also come over to my house to read and play with my youngest, Danielle, when she was a baby, or when I needed some free time at home to nap or take a long hot shower and put my feet up for an hour of uninterrupted time. That time was heaven for me. Today we call it "self-care." Find a trusted young person to be your youth support. It can be invaluable help for you as a mom, and the student can use the time as community service.

Being my children's mentor, Marguerite wanted to do whatever her mentor Helene did. I would take Marguerite to see Helene at school for activities and events which allowed Marguerite to see opportunities available to her. For example, Helene was the first of my friend's group of children to attend boarding school for high school as an A Better Chance scholar. After watching Helene accomplish this, Marguerite was determined to be an ABC scholar and attend boarding school as well. She did and, even more, attended on a full scholarship.

Similarly, a young man from our church, Michell, befriended Darryl. Darryl always felt like an outsider to other students who did not have an Individual Education Plan (IEP) for students with disabilities. Other students knew there was something different about him, but in most cases, did not know what. He looked like any other tall, handsome boy. However, he did not always understand them and what they did. So, he was shunned by most. However, Michell always included Darryl in discussions at church and Sunday School, and reached out to him with a greeting whenever he saw him. As a result, the other children did the same. Michell also came over to our house to hang out with Darryl. This gave him a sense of belonging, acceptance and confidence.

It is important that parents help prepare their child to pursue the things they are interested in. Help them determine what their goals are by getting them involved in activities, like girl scouts, boys scouts, judo, track and field, and tutoring other children. Find a trusted young person to be a mentor, someone they can relate to, who is kind and not judgmental.

If your child is struggling in school, find a tutor for them. If you don't have the money, find a young person who will tutor your child for community service. Helene tutored the girls for community service, and I also paid her. In addition, I paid for a tutoring service to prepare my children to take the SSAT for private school and math tutors throughout middle and high school, and the SAT for college. The higher their scores were, the more scholarship money they would receive.

CHAPTER SIX

WORLD TRAVEL

I'm one of those parents who likes to volunteer with organizations to broaden my horizons and find opportunities for children. I have always wanted my children to have travel abroad opportunities and meet students from other countries. My mother gave me that opportunity when I was fifteen years old. She saved $200 – a lot of money for her in the 1970s – to allow me to travel with a teacher and two other high school students to Port au Prince, Haiti. This experience gave me the travel bug. Since then, I've had the opportunity to travel abroad to five continents through my career and as an exchange student program volunteer.

One such opportunity came when I volunteered with an organization that needed American families to host exchange students from China. We hosted a young boy from China first, then later on, three girls from China. My daughter, Danielle, was eleven years old when we hosted our first exchange student. She decided she wanted to learn Mandarin so she could talk to the exchange students. I did some research and was told to contact a professor in Asian studies at Georgetown.

I called the professor who requested that I bring Danielle in to meet with her. She was so impressed that Danielle was interested in learning Mandarin that she gave her a gift from China and told me about a Mandarin class for children near my home. Danielle and I visited the class and she decided right there she wanted to enroll. She was the oldest student in the class at eleven years old. Most of the students were ages five to seven. She was determined to catch up to the younger kids, some of whom had already been taking Mandarin for a year. The class was for ten weeks on Sundays so I took her after church and she did well.

My family went on to host students from Egypt, Lebanon, and Turkey. I also became a volunteer with the State Department foreign exchange program and found American host families for exchange students. This allowed me to become familiar with exchange programs for American students as well.

Marguerite's first all-expense-paid travel abroad program was to Spain for one month with Experiment in International Living (EIL) while she was in high school. She went on to travel to South Africa, Turkey – she taught English to Turkish children for two summers – as well as Trinidad and Tobago on a scholarship. Danielle had an opportunity to travel abroad to Kazakhstan on her first travel abroad trip at the age of thirteen, to accompany me as I was a flight leader, escorting exchange students back to their home country after a school year in the U.S. living with American families. I requested approval for her to go with me as a teen flight leader and my request was approved. It was the first time a teen had been approved to serve as a flight leader, and it was also the first time anyone had asked.

She went on to apply and was selected for the very competitive, State Department funded, National Security Language Initiative for Youth (NSLI-Y). NSLI-Y is an outstanding language program for high school students to learn a critical language as classified by the Department of State while abroad for a summer program. The program was six weeks, or a school year and there is no language requirement. My daughter was selected for the six-week program in China. She was fortunate to know some Mandarin when she went, as she also studied it in middle and high school, although there were several students in her group of 30 high school students who did not know Mandarin who were also selected.

I've counseled and mentored several families on how to apply to fully funded, or partially funded, study abroad programs. One of my mentees spent a month in Greece, and others went to Kenya and Europe. I mentored some families on fundraising for the programs that did not offer scholarships suggesting they be creative with their fundraiser. One family hosted a community festival in her backyard netting her $1,000. I told her to seek out local business sponsorships by putting together her daughter's resume/brag sheet. It worked, as it has also worked for me and other families I've worked with over the years.

If you had told me 20 years ago that my children would be traveling the world, I would never have believed you. Our culture and society have always dictated a predetermined route for our lives: getting good grades in school, then getting a job, getting married, having children and going on vacation once a year. However, my children have been to China, Kazakhstan, Cuba, Panama, Spain, South Africa, Turkey, Trinidad, and Thailand, just to name a few—mostly on scholarship programs.

There are far more opportunities for children seeking out a more diverse population then there were when I was a child. There are so many resources at our disposal to break the mold and live the life we've always dreamed of for our children. And not one is dictated by what society expects of you, outside of entertainment and sports. African Americans can, and are, traveling the world. The world is the textbook and the classroom. I have helped students and inspired them to get scholarships because of my children's travel abroad opportunities. These students are truly getting a real world-class education, all over the world.

Today, many folks are making careers out of being digital nomads, living and traveling the world outside the United States or their home country. Who knew then, that there would be social media platforms allowing people to travel to the furthest corner of the earth and become citizens of the world? My daughter was living in the Republic of Panama, blogging and vlogging about her experience for college credit. There are several scholarships available for travel abroad for foreign students to come to the USA and for American students to go abroad or experience virtual travel abroad during COVID-19.

When Marguerite participated in the Experiment in International Living (EIL) program for a month, she was able to explore Barcelona, Madrid, and Toledo. It included staying with a host family and in hotels in Barcelona and Madrid. The program taught students about the differences in cultures across Spain's distinct regions as they interacted with the locals and learned Spanish. It was her first travel abroad experience at the age of sixteen, paid for with a scholarship.

I've mentored many students over the years. One of my former mentees was selected to go to Greece when she was sixteen years old for a month on a scholarship after I recommended her for the study abroad program. The program only required that a student have a 2.5 GPA or higher. She was a delightful young lady from my church that a friend recommended to me. She did not have a high GPA, but she had a great attitude and she excelled in the program. She has recently been selected to several PhD candidate programs and has credited me with helping her realize her destiny. There are several scholarship programs for students who don't have a high GPA. All students have an opportunity to excel and be included in great programs with a variety of interests.

Additionally, travel abroad starts long before you get on a plane. Even now, some are traveling during COVID-19, right from their couch. How do you travel the world from your couch? Well, like many people, we have had to hit pause on our travel plans for the time being, but that doesn't mean we're not still thinking about all the places we've been, and all the places we hope to go sometime soon. After all, so much of travel trickles into our lives both before and after a big trip, whether it is the hours we spend scouring the internet for inspiration on where to go next. Places influence us long after we've left, through the food we cook to the souvenirs we fill our homes with to the music we listen to. Travel first starts in your imagination. Where do you want to go? Here is some information to get you started:

Editors, CNT. "101 Ways to Travel Without Leaving Your House." Condé Nast Traveler, 20 Mar. 2020, www.cntraveler.com/story/101-ways-to-travel-without-leaving-your-house.

Marguerite in Istanbul Turkey with her College on a scholarship to teach Turkish youth English

Danielle with friend in Tiananmen Square, China on scholarship for the U.S. Department of State

CHAPTER SEVEN

DON'T LET A DISABILITY DIMINISH EXPECTATIONS OF WHAT YOUR CHILD CAN ACCOMPLISH

Over the years, I have had to battle with schools or organizations that are supposed to work on behalf of students with disabilities. One case in point was when Darryl was eleven years old. He was selected to participate in a summer camp for students with disabilities who liked working on computers. One of his teachers told me about the program and recommended I apply for him. It was a great program. The program was at the Helen A. Keller Institute for Human disAbilities at George Mason University. They were developing a pilot computer program to help students learn math and reading based on their individual abilities. The director of the camp was impressed with Darryl's progress using the program and informed me that he would benefit from having a laptop at home to ensure his continued success at school and home. She told me there was funding to assist disabled students with technology by helping them get a personal laptop from the school system.

I left with a better sense of how this would help my son. After talking to my son's special education teacher, she set up an appointment with the PhD in charge of the assistive technology program for the school district. I had my memo and backup material that supported my request for the laptop. I told her the story about the summer program my son had successfully completed, how I found out about the assistive technology program and how a dedicated laptop for Darryl would help him with his lessons. The expert listened to me, but never looked at any of the material I brought with me, and then said no.

Putting on my Warrior Mom persona, I paused looking her in the eye. I pulled out the school system's budget for assistive technology that showed $12,000 set aside for the assistive program. I lost my cool, telling her if she was going to refuse my request, then at least read it, and put her disapproval in writing. I would take it from there. I asked her where the money was, since her own budget showed the money had never been spent on assistive technology. My son's teacher, who knew me well, was shocked at how I went after the expert. She looked down at the floor the whole time while I went on my rant. After the meeting, she said, "Mrs. Lyle, I've never seen you like that." I told her there was no reason for her to see me like that before. The next day, my son had his laptop with all the programs on it I requested.

Darryl kept the computer throughout high school with the school's IT staff updating it with programs he needed over the years. When Darryl graduated, we returned the laptop back to the school system. The teacher asked me how I got the information about the budget. I told her I first asked my son's school principal for the information, and she said I would have to go to the county school level to request it. I did that and they refused to provide me with the information. I then went online to the Virginia Department of Education, found six names on their website of people who worked in special education. I sent them each individual emails requesting information about how much money was set aside for students with disabilities for assistive technology. One person responded with a spreadsheet that outlined all the funding for the entire school system.

As a parent, you are your children's first and best advocate. Do not ever let anyone make you feel small and powerless with their PhD degrees in whatever. Ask for what you want, in writing, and don't take no for an answer when you know it's something that can be done. No one will care more about your child than you. Become a pest. Teachers, and others, would see me coming and go the other way. I followed them and, most of the time, I was very polite but I was relentless. I kept after them until I got what I wanted. However, do your homework.

"Don't accept a No from anyone who is not authorized to say Yes."

Rhonda Copeland Lyle

I also recommend that you try to get the answer to your question before you even ask. I typically know the person can do what I'm requesting before I ask. Even if I do not know the answer, I would make them do their research to tell me no with documentation. Several teachers told me that they were encouraged to say no to anything a parent asked because most parents would accept the no and move on. If you are asking for something doable, do not give up.

When Danielle applied for her Congressional Gold Medal for Youth, the requirement was for the students to have 400 hours of community service, 200 hours of self-development, 200 hours of athletics and a five-day exploration over at least a two-year period or more, after the registration date for the program. She far exceeded the requirement for community service by 200 hours, and athletics by 100 hours. After Danielle submitted her paperwork for approval, the program manager responsible for the approval and for forwarding her documentation to the full board for approval challenged how she could have accrued so many hours at her school, especially for athletics. He sent her an email accusing her of lying in her documentation, although the paperwork was validated by the school advisor and her validator in each area. She called me from her boarding school as she had no time to call them personally.

She sent the young man an email requesting that he contact her validator for proof. Then I, Warrior Mom, had to fight another battle. I emailed the man, scolding him for accusing her of lying without first requesting clarification. I told him that obviously he was used to reviewing public school students' applications, where certain athletics are only conducted at certain times of the year. However, my daughter's school programs were conducted all year long and in the summer. I copied his boss, and they both apologized for the "mix-up." My daughter received her gold medal on time with other students from around the country in a wonderful gala on Capitol Hill in Washington DC. If they didn't approve her application, she would have had to wait another year.

I always looked for programs that fostered self-esteem, leadership, academic excellence, empowerment, and community service with other fun things my children liked doing. I advise you to do the same. When your children are having fun while learning, it is the best possible combination for growth and advancement.

I helped a colleague determine outlets for her four year old son, who had recently been diagnosed with a learning disability. She and her husband were devastated by the news. I told her my son was also in special education at school, and I asked if she really believed her son had a learning disability. As parents of African American boys, we know how some in the school system quickly want to label them in a negative way. Schools often put African American boy students in special education to get more money for the school, and then use it for other things, not special education. The goal is to ensure your child has well-rounded experiences as they develop their interests, so you can then focus on building expertise in special education or programs for the gifted.

I advised her that everything she did with him should be to help him learn through study and fun activities that would develop his ability to think critically, comprehend, be self-confident and proud of who he is as a Black male. He is six years old now and loves art and creative activities. Determine what your child is most interested in and give him or her opportunities to be exposed to and use those things.

Create a resume for your child now. I was able to help build my children's resumes by doing activities with them. If being an alpha, Warrior Mom means that I involve myself in raising my children by ensuring they have opportunities, communicating with teachers to demand they get a good education, advocating for them, and ensuring they are not ignored when opportunities become available, then I am a proud alpha parent and make no apology for it.

In my opinion, more parents need to be actively involved in their children's lives. Be a parent, you are not their friend. You are responsible for keeping them safe and ensuring their friends and their families are like-minded. The reason the book club worked so well for so long was because I only invited like-minded families to be in the group.

I hear parents say their children will not let them take their phone from them. Who pays the bill? Let them keep the phone if you like, but suspend the service so they cannot use it. Stand your ground. You are in charge. They are children, they don't know any better, though still make sure you listen to their opinions. But remember, you make the final decision based on your knowledge and experience. Do not be afraid to say no to your child. As my friend says, "No is a complete sentence." It will be to their advantage and they will appreciate it when they are older, as my adult children do today. My children were not always happy with the things that I made them be involved in. However, after they went off to college, they realized they had a lot more experiences than their peers of the same age.

My children were ordinary children for whom extraordinary experiences were able to open doors and provide opportunities for them. In the movie, Slumdog Millionaire, a street kid in India wins $1 million on a game show. He had no formal education, though he had life of experiences on the streets where he picked up information about a variety of things that educated him. The police arrested him because they thought he somehow cheated to win the million dollars. They could not understand how a street kid could possibly know so much about the world. Now, I am not saying that children should be on the streets to learn and become experienced. The movie was a drama – just fiction. However, find and give your child opportunities. Do not just be satisfied with the status quo. Think outside the box.

Raising children to become healthy, thriving adults isn't about clearing adversity out of their way. It is about nurturing their mindsets, self-esteem, and inner strength. It's also about giving them strategies to deal with tough situations and teaching them to get up after they fall again and again.

CHAPTER EIGHT

DO EVERYTHING YOU CAN TO HELP YOUR CHILD SUCCEED

10 Keys to Growing a Brilliant Child from Birth to Adulthood

(Author Unknown)

1. Start as early as possible: Start now. Whatever your child's age is, do not delay. If your child is a newborn, it is a perfect time to start. If your child is a teenager, it is not too late. As parents, it is our privilege and our obligation to take care of our children's education. Now is the best time to start.
2. Make it fun. For children, learning is fun. What does a child do when he plays with his toys? He is diligently learning about his environment. If you observe a young child playing with his toys, you can see that when he has completed learning all that he can get from a toy, he tosses it aside and looks for a new one! Keep it light and fun. This will ensure that your child grows up to be a lifelong learner.

3. You are your child's natural teacher. No matter how many teachers your child has or will have in school and outside of school, you are his first and most important teacher. Take advantage of this and make sure you teach your child valuable lessons.
4. We all underestimate the ability of children to learn. When babies cannot speak, we do not know how much they can learn. We do not know how much they can understand. But this is a very valuable period of time. At this time, your child is learning his mother tongue. At this time, your child has an amazing talent to recognize patterns. You can take advantage of this important period of time to teach your child many things related to language skills, like vocabulary, reading and more.
5. If you expose children to many subjects and activities, they will show you what they are interested in. Then you can take advantage of those interests and relate other subjects to them. Let your children lead the way.
6. Children hate to be tested. Never test your child or learning will stop being fun for him. Trust that whatever learning activity you are doing with your child is successful. Trust that your child is learning. Never doubt that. When it is the right time, your child will show you how much he learned.
7. Children learn much faster than we adults do. If you want to keep your young child interested; you have to move at your child's speed—fast.
8. Your child's self-confidence and self-esteem are most important. Look for things to praise him for and avoid criticism. Every day when your child goes to bed, discuss the day's events, and mention all the successes and achievements of the day. Get into the habit of doing this; it will make a big difference in your child's confidence.
9. Teach your child to set goals early on. Set yearly, monthly, weekly, and daily goals. Teach your child how to put together a plan, and how to change the plan when it is necessary. At the end of the year, celebrate the child's achievements. Make sure your child knows how successful he is.

10. Make sure your child knows that it is OK to make mistakes. It is OK to try and fail. Failure is just a learning opportunity, a signal to try a different way. A child who knows this will not be discouraged or give up. A child who knows this lesson will keep a healthy self-esteem and confidence in spite of occasional setbacks.

The more you teach your child, the stronger the bond between you. As you watch your child develop, succeed, and meet their own goals, the memories you are creating together will turn into the dearest memories in your child's life, and in your own.

> *"There is a brilliant child locked inside every student,"*
> **- Marva Collins**

Marva Collins was an American educator who broke off from a public school system she found to be failing inner city children and established her own school with a rigorous system and practice to cultivate her students' independence and accomplishments. She started her school in Chicago, called Westside Prep. In 1979 Westside Prep gained national prominence following a story and interview with Collins on the television show, 60 Minutes. In 1981, CBS aired the Marva Collins Story. Mrs. Collins refused several offers for powerful positions, including U.S. Secretary of Education. In 2004 President George W. Bush awarded Collins the prestigious National Humanities Medal.

I had the pleasure of meeting Mrs. Collins in 2006 when she was a guest teacher trainer at my oldest daughter's school. Marguerite's school, Pennington School, was a public school that operated like a private school. It was a much sought-after school that was an alternative to the traditional public school. The students were tested and had to go through a lottery system to be admitted. My daughter was fortunate to be accepted, and transferred to Pennington from a private school, Cardinal Montessori, for fifth grade. I learned about the teacher training with Mrs. Collins and decided to invite myself. I had read one of her books, Ordinary Children, Extraordinary Teachers.

The training was extraordinary. The teachers got a lot out of it, and so did I, even though I am not a teacher. How was I able to attend, you ask? I just showed up. I did not give the administration the opportunity to say no. If they turned me away, so be it. I did not lose anything, but gained a lot from the meeting and being taught by a titan teacher

Be an activist parent. Do not ask permission to learn all you can to help your child be successful. Just show up!

"Nothing changes until you take action."
~Mia Redrick, Business and Life Coach

CHAPTER NINE

BE YOUR CHILD'S BEST ADVOCATE

Over the years, I have been invited to speak to parents at various venues addressing how parents can, and should, advocate for their child. At one event, a parent shared with me and the group that her daughter was given a failing grade for not turning in a paper, although her daughter had indeed turned the paper in. When the mother contacted the teacher to ask her to check her files again, and that her daughter did the paper – the mother and daughter had a copy of the paper and turned it into the teacher again – the teacher refused to talk to the parent, telling her the middle school child was responsible for advocating for herself, not the parent. The child had already spoken to the teacher, who dismissed her without acknowledging that the paper had been turned in. The mother shared that she was intimidated by the teacher, and let the incident go. She asked me what she should do.

The story made my blood boil. I told the parent to make an appointment with the school principal, take a copy of the paper, and get her child the credit she deserves. I also told her to tell the school principal that she wanted to ensure that no reprisals were perpetrated against her daughter by the teacher or anyone else at the school.

Parents, ensure your children receive credit for everything they do. Teachers are not infallible, they make mistakes. Help them help your child. Most teachers will be happy for the support from parents when done in a respectful manner. However, when they don't help your child, do not be afraid to challenge them for the good of your child.

Remember, you are the first advocate for your child. There is always a way. Make the investment to get your child the kind of education that will change, broaden and inspire their life-long desire to be global, educated citizens, wherever they are and no matter the background, income, ability or disAbility.

Allow your child to grow and experience things you, or they, would never consider. Take them to the library and read about different subjects like space, diving, the art of fencing, topics they see on television, and that are safe and appropriate. Give them flexibility.

Parents, be alert, aware, and demand excellence from the educational systems.
~Rhonda Copeland Lyle

Finally, as you grow in your understanding of the opportunities available to your child, understanding the financial aspects of their educational journey is also key. It is important to have elevated conversations with your children about how to manage their finances, so they are not saddled with debt as they begin their adult lives.

Throughout this book, I referred to my three children, Darryl, Marguerite and Danielle. The two older children are actually my niece and nephew. We raised them from the age of 9 and 6 years old, respectfully. Danielle does not know what it is like to be an only child, thank God! I was a full-time working mom. Although, it was not easy we did our best to give all the kids opportunities.

They are now adults, living their lives and doing well. I don't share this to get a pat on the back, but to encourage families to step in and care for your family's children when possible. The system is filled with children in foster care, and many with no one who really cares about them.

CHAPTER TEN

CONCLUSION

In my 20 years of researching, asking questions, eavesdropping on others' conversations who did not want to share great information and opportunities they knew about with me – including teachers, administrators, and other parents – I found there were enough opportunities to go around, and was bent on sharing and helping as many families as I could, especially black families. Many of the families would say they never heard of the programs.

This book is my labor of love. Its' mission is to consolidate the work I've done in finding and getting opportunities and scholarships for my children and other students and families. It has been my joy to share them with many other families, and now I get to share them with you. My true passion is helping children realize their greatness through opportunities.

Throughout my children's' education and travels, I was a full-time working mom. Although it was not easy, we did our best to give them each ample opportunities. They are now adults, living their lives as college graduates, in college, and doing well. I do not share this to get a pat on the back, but to encourage families to do everything possible to help their children, including stepping in to support and care for any extended family children when needed.

I also want to encourage parents to not let the world set expectations for your child. They often set a low bar, especially for students of color. You get to set the bar high for your child, including children with disabilities, and teach them to set a high bar for themselves as well.

Someone posted on Facebook in 2019 on the page, My Cozy Cups, saying, "a good education begins at home. You cannot blame a school for not nurturing values in your child that you have not instilled." Take the lead when your child is younger. Your child will benefit greatly from it and be able to lead themselves when they need to, based on your example.

Parents, you will have to learn to lead and advocate from behind when your child goes off to college. They still need guidance, so you will have to adjust your approach for them to receive it as young adults. They are on their own and will choose the voices they listen to. Many parents automatically think that when their children go off to college, they have to be hands-off. I was not hands-off. I communicated with professors and was listed to have access to grade information. You are still their parents and they are still teenagers when they first leave, and there is more life learning needed, but you are leading from behind.

Our children are the future. They are taking on the leadership roles in the country. Feel good about the opportunities you have given them. They will have challenges but do all you can to give them the wisdom to make good decisions, and when they don't, to pick themselves up, brush themselves off, and keep moving upward.

I hope this book provides you with insight and inspires what you and your child can do to find and get great opportunities and scholarships. This can be used for anything you want to do in life. You don't need a lot of money, just the desire to provide for your children, family, and the community.

SOME LETTERS OF RECOMMENDATIONS OVER THE YEARS

Conclusion

From: **Rhonda Lyle** lyle.rhonda5@gmail.com
Subject: **A thank you note**
Date: **Apr 23, 2020 at 2:36:17 PM**
To: **Rhonda Lyle** lyle.rhonda5@gmail.com

From Stacey Burnard 4/15/2020
Hello Rhonda I wanted to reach out to you and just say hello. During this crazy time of Covid, I want say hello, I thought of you today and I prayed for you! You have been a blessing to so many and touched many lives to include mine and Madison's! You are appreciated and I want to say thank you! Often times we forget to say these things while we still have the opportunity. May God continue to bless you and show you favor!

Have a super fantastic and blessed day! Stay safe!
Stacey Burnard

Sent from my iPhone

J. Nelson

May 28, 2015

Spelman College Youth Summer Program

To Whom It May Concern:

This letter is intended as a professional recommendation for Mrs. Rhonda Lyle. For the past four years, I have been Rhonda's client and friend. Rhonda not only assisted with our son's acceptance to the A Better Chance Program, however, she continues to serve as a valuable resource. She has provided recommendations and advice about academic and leadership programs such as ARMY Gains in Engineering Math and Science (GEMS). Currently, our son is in the eighth grade at one of the most prestigious independent schools in the DC Metro Area. In addition, he has been accepted into top notch boarding schools for High School, is a Johns Hopkins Center for Talented Youth Young Scholar and an A Better Chance Young Leader Recipient. We would not have gotten to this point without her assistance.

Rhonda has taken the time to get to know our son over the years so that she can offer sound advice and recommendations based on what she considers the best fit for him. Her personal care and individualized attention to her clients are unlike no other and it shows. She has assisted many students who go on to achieve great success.

I have been thoroughly impressed with both her professionalism and performance in the field of Academic enrichment. I look forward to continuing to work with her throughout our son's High School and College years. With Rhonda by our side, I know our son will continue to SOAR.

I wholeheartedly recommend Rhonda as a consultant for the Summer Youth Program. She would be a valuable asset to any organization. I am happy to answer any additional questions you may have and can be reached at

Sincerely,

Joi Nelson, Esq.

Conclusion

28 July 2014

SUBJECT: Letter of Character Reference, Mrs. Rhonda Lyle

TO WHOM IT MAY CONCERN:

It is my pleasure to submit this letter of character reference for a dear friend of over 20 years.

I first met Rhonda as a neighbor. As time transformed our lives into being spouses and mothers, I was introduced, continually, to a person who is benevolent, determined, intelligent, selfless, honest, spiritual, committed, resourceful, loyal, encouraging and charitable, to name a few personal attributes. I use these words to describe her because they are true to HER core. Her life is a prime example of my description of her and she lives to make a difference, not only, in her personal life, but also, in the lives of many family members and friends.

Rhonda's commitment to her family is outstanding. Not being married for very long, Rhonda and her husband, Lionel, made the choice to seek and gain custody of her, elementary age, niece and nephew. She recognized that these kids were in an environment that did not promote safety, stability, opportunity, education and care. The welfare of her niece and nephew far outweighed the new life she had begun with her husband and all of the financial and physical freedoms that a childless marriage, at that time, would bring. The old saying, "charity starts at home," is truly embodied in this family's lifestyle. After having their own child, Rhonda and Lyle, over the years, committed to care for another niece, brother, father and mother. With that level of commitment to her family, while working full-time, she continued to seek ways to provide enhancements to the lives of her friends and friends' children.

In 2003, Rhonda was instrumental in starting a children's book club. The purpose of the book club was to teach and introduce the kids to books that added another dimension of communication, comprehension and creative thinking. The book club members also participated in activities outside the norm of what a book club does. The kids were challenged with public speaking, completing projects, hosting political fund raisers and participating in community services. They attended various life enhancement programs, such as, a symposium with Dr. Ben Carson of John Hopkins Hospital in Baltimore, Maryland and in-depth, appropriate-age, counseling sessions regarding sexual education to include abstinence, sexual diseases, consequences of sexual behavior, etc. This level of enrichment for our kids have proven to be one of the best development tools the kids have experienced. It served as a foundation for their desire to be better and do better for themselves, as well as, for others. The successes and goals attained by the kids today, can be directly attributable to the varied opportunities afforded them as a "Future Leaders Book Club" member.

Other entities have been blessed from the deeds and aspirations of Rhonda's. She and her husband have participated, as hosts, in the exchange student program and Rhonda has been instrumental in providing help in finding sponsors for other exchange students.

Rhonda Copeland Lyle

Her passion and compassion for children run deep. It is her desire to see that every child has the same opportunities that her children have been afforded. Through hard work, perseverance and no excuses, Rhonda believes that the short-sightedness that some people have for a certain class, nationality or race of people can be obliterated. At some level, all kids want to be productive God-fearing adults and it's up to us to help them achieve their goals.

A lot of what Rhonda has accomplished working with different nationalities of children were as a full-time working mom, aunt and wife. Now that she has retired, niece and nephew graduated from college and a daughter on the brink of graduating from high school, her level of, an already high commitment to children, is even greater. Rhonda believes in our youth and their potential. Unquestionably, our youths' desires, goals and achievements should be the forefront of any plan that encourages and promotes excellence. She has proven over and over, it's not about her, it's the children who are the driving force behind her actions.

If you have any questions, please feel free to contact me

Sincerely,

Cassandra Wins

Conclusion

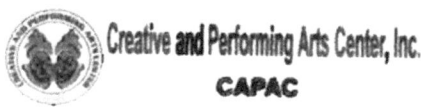

Loretta Freeman

To Whom It May Concern,

My name is Loretta Freeman and I serve as President of the Creative and Performing Arts Center (CAPAC). I have had the extreme pleasure to know and work with Rhonda Lyle in many facets over the past eleven years. Ms. Lyle has imparted effective academic support to me and my family in both a professional and personal capacity. It is an honor to provide Rhonda with this personal letter of reference/recommendation.

It is a gifted person who takes the time to see the potential in all children. Rhonda has the passion to bring their talents to the surface. She advocates for them to focus on their highest goal while meticulously searching for resources that will benefit their academic advancement. Rhonda, through raising her daughter, niece and nephew, has developed knowledge and expertise in matching opportunities available and she unselfishly shares these valuable assets with others.

Rhonda is a truly dedicated individual. When she decides what her mission will be, she is totally committed and zeroes in at all cost until the mission is considered complete. Rhonda has provided tremendous support and encouragement for CAPAC either personally, via her family or other organizations in which she is affiliated. She will be an essential asset in any endeavor that she joins.

Should any additional information be required, please feel free to contact me

Sincerely,

Loretta Freeman

Loretta Freeman

Post Office Box 4970, Woodbridge, Virginia 22194   www.capacweb.org   703-441-2479

Rhonda Copeland Lyle

To Whom It May Concern,

    I am writing this letter on behalf of Mrs. Rhonda Lyle. I have known Rhonda for over 10 years and in that time; Rhonda has shown herself to be a passionate and dedicated person regarding children and youth academic and social development. Rhonda was a founding member of the African American Children's Book Club. The purpose of the club was to expose children to books written by African American writers while fostering a love of reading. In addition, the book club served to enhance the public speaking skills of the members as well an awareness of cultural experiences outside of their realm. Rhonda organized and created activities and field trips related to the books or themes suggested for the children to take part. In 2011 as the children were transitioning from middle school to High School, Rhonda decided to take the book club and transform it into an organization that would provide support for the members as they transitioned into high school. Out of her desire to ensure that the members would succeed academically, and to lay seeds of development and growth for their future endeavors, Rhonda created The Future Leader s Club..

The Future Leaders Club provided an opportunity for the youth to create events that mattered to them. They discussed issues that impacted their lives and used their own voices when participating in the various and continuous events and activities that they were a part of. Rhonda became an advocate and facilitator. She continued to facilitate programs such as SAT prep courses designed for each child's individual need, math and language tutoring camps as well as Science and Technology camps for the children to attend. She helped them as they decided to participate in their very first fundraiser for a presidential election. She has advocated for them through recommendations for high school and academic achievement programs and has encouraged them to participate in writing and literacy projects including publishing books and interviewing historical figures.

Mrs. Rhonda Lyle is a parent and an advocate for all children she comes in contact with. She wants as much for them as she does for her own children. She pushes all parents to achieve academic success for their own children as well. She operates from the motto of one child's success is all of our success. Rhonda's joy is watching the children she comes into contact with blossom and become confident and talented individuals and Future Leaders for tomorrow.

It has been my pleasure and honor befriending Rhonda and I am glad to recommend her for any position as a youth advocate.

Sincerely,

Dorothy Gaspard-St.Cyr

Conclusion

Sandra Manigault, M.A.

July 28, 2014

To whom it may concern:

This letter is in support of Mrs. Rhonda Lyle who is applying to be a court-appointed child advocate in the Commonwealth of Virginia. In the many years that I have known and worked with Mrs. Lyle, I have been most impressed with the ardor with which she has advocated for the educational enhancement of children. Although there are many parents who advocate for their own children, Mrs. Lyle not only searches out the very best opportunities for her children, but for the children of many, many other parents as well.

Mrs. Lyle is very well educated, extremely knowledgeable, ambitious for the well being of children, detail-oriented, and dependable. She has been an advocate for many students to become admitted to the A Better Chance Program, which selects outstanding minority students for private and boarding schools in the United States. She has contributed much to the children of her community, including starting a children's book club, hosting a Summer Math and Art Camp, engaging children in the political process, hosting opportunities for children to meet and host dignitaries, such as the sister of Archbishop Desmond Tutu, and others, and most importantly, making parents aware of the many, many supplementary educational opportunities for children that are available in the Washington D.C. area and nationwide. She has also hosted and supervised international students through various programs through the U.S. Department of State.

Her own children have exemplified excellence on many levels, to include playing several musical instruments, winning oratorical contests, participating in numerous leadership conferences, publishing a very significant first book, travel abroad to Spain, China, Turkey and South Africa; being recognized by the President for their community service, and so much more. Frequently I tell friends and associates, that her younger daughter alone, at the age of 17, has a resume that would surpass that of many adult professionals three times her age.

There is no doubt in my mind that Rhonda Lyle would be an outstanding child advocate, and that any child who is privileged to work with her will have his or her life changed in countless ways for the better.

Thank you.

Sincerely yours,

Sandra Manigault
Sandra Manigault

Kathy Wilson

January 7, 2012

To Whom It May Concern,

I have known Rhonda Lyle for the past eight years. We worship at the same church and have worked together on a number of successful projects during that time.

Rhonda is organized, efficient, extremely competent, and has an excellent rapport with people of all ages. Rhonda founded the Future Leaders Book Club to which my 12 year old daughter has been a member since age four. The book club, a small group of hand selected children and their "Hands -on" parents, is much more than your typical book-club. The children meet quarterly to read, write about, and orally present on a variety of books. With Rhonda's leadership, I've watched these often initially shy four and five year olds, blossom into strong, confident, high achieving young people.

Rhonda's passion for enriching the lives of children goes well beyond the confines of your traditional book club. She has researched and exposed not only the book-club kids, but many many others into participating in a number of academic enrichment programs to include:

1) **A better Chance (ABC):** A program whose mission is to expose academically talented youth of color to greater educational opportunities;

2) Gains in Engineering & Mathematics (GEMS): A program designed to engage and guide students and teachers in science, technology, engineering and mathematics (STEM) education;

3) **Johns Hopkins Center for Talented Youth:** A program designed to identify, challenge, and reward academically able young people;

4) **Junior Youth Leaders Conference:** A program that helps scholars develop and sharpen their leadership skills by examining the leaders of the past and empowering them to make a positive social impact in their community and the world.

These four tremendous opportunities are just a sampling of the programs that Rhonda has introduced to the book club kids and countless other children and their parents. The most personally unselfish and quite possibly the most challenging endeavor was Rhonda's commitment to taking in and providing a home for her niece and nephew; both of whom were of early elementary school age when her care for them began. Her nephew Darryl at the time was

Conclusion

diagnosed a "Special Needs Child" and came with all of the challenges therewith. Most people would have found this task daunting, but not Rhonda. While also working a full time job, she made it her personal mission to provide a loving home and transform their lives into the accomplished young adults that they are today. Darryl, who was told would never read, nor overcome extreme behavioral problems, now works and attends college courses at George Mason University. Under Rhonda's tutelage, Marguerite, Rhonda's niece has flourished and grown up to be one of the most accomplished young people I know. Not only did she participate in and excel in all of the many academic enrichment programs listed above and more, she has traveled abroad several times, and received academic scholarships from a very prestigious boarding school called Oldfields in Maryland; where she was class president and graduated with honors. Marguerite currently attends Wheaton College on full academic scholarship.

Rhonda did all of this while raising her own daughter Danielle who has a remarkable collection of her own outstanding scholar accolades. Danielle is only 14 years old, but is an honors student at St Timothy's boarding school in Maryland. Rhonda commissioned me to create a memory book for Danielle and her very impressive accomplishments won't even fit into the book for this, the early chapters of Danielle's life.

Rhonda has recruited and encouraged young people of all ages to not only excel academically, but to prepare resumes/biographies filled with many other "Rhonda Lyle inspired and organized": Community service events (i.e. canvassing for the 2008 Obama Presidential Campaign, and planning, hosting and performing in an Inaugural Gala for President Obama for an attendance of over 80 people; hosting a reception to support Dr. Luke E. Torian for delegate of the 52nd District of Northern Va, and Creigh Deeds for Governor, to name a few). She has also organized field trips to John Hopkins Hospital in Baltimore MD for the children to meet the world renowned Neural Surgeon Dr. Ben Carson; along with countless trips to the Kennedy Center in Washington D.C. for additional cultural enrichment experiences though the arts and theatre. The children have taken etiquette classes, SSAT prep classes, investment seminars, and participated in Genealogy seminars to learn the importance of knowing their heritage, all at the encouragement and recommendation of Rhonda Lyle.

In summary, I have only scratched the surface of the numerous accomplishments and opportunities from which countless children have benefited, for which Rhonda Lyle can take credit. But she won't, she is just that humble. You will never hear her brag or ask for anything in return. She loves inspiring and nurturing young people, and she does it with an unmatched passion, and unparalleled dedication and commitment to the children. I highly recommend Rhonda for any position or endeavor that she may seek to pursue. She will be a valuable asset to any organization.

If you have any questions, please do not hesitate to contact me.

Sincerely,

Kathy Wilson

Kathy Wilson

EPILOGUE

As you read this story, many people have told me they think I did some amazing things. However, this is my story, and you have your own powerful story. I know this may not work for every household but do what you can that works for your family. I made some career choices that were best for my family, as well as some sacrifices. I had a great job working and travelling abroad during my time at the Pentagon, which I loved. The folks I worked with were amazing, and the best group of people I had ever worked with. However, I made the decision to transfer to another organization that I knew I would not like but did so anyway for the flexibility I would have. This was a choice I made to be closer to home and which required no travel. By doing this, I was able to participate in my children's school programs, go on school trips, volunteer at school, etc. When opportunities presented themselves, I was able to drop everything and take off work to gather up the children, and other book club children, to have them participate in once in a lifetime opportunities, like meeting Supreme Court Justice Sonia Sotomayor with only three hours' notice, and Princess Nancy's visit from Swaziland. I decided not to seek any more promotions, and just retired early when I became eligible. I never looked back and am now living my best life, once again travelling the world and living abroad for a while. I delayed my gratification for my children and I'm so glad I did.

> "*Success awaits those who steadfastly commit to any requisite sacrificed.*"
>
> **- Ken Poirot**

A SHORT LISTING OF OPPORTUNITIES FOR STUDENTS

– Compiled by Rhonda Lyle

A Better Chance (ABC)
The College Preparatory Schools Program (CPSP) nationally recruits, places, and supports students enrolled in grades fourth through ninth at more than 300 independent day, boarding, and select public schools.
https://www.abetterchance.org/admissions-and-programming/admissions-cycle/scholars

Gains in Education, Math and Science (GEMS)
Program pays students in grades fifth through ninth to attend. GEMS' mission is to interest young people who might not otherwise give serious thought to becoming scientists or engineers, in STEM careers early enough that they have the time to attain the appropriate academic training. https://www.usaeop.com/program/gems/

U.S. Government Student Aid for College and Career Schools
Scholarships are gifts. They don't need to be repaid. There are thousands of them, offered by schools, employers, individuals, private companies, nonprofits, communities, religious groups, and professional and social organizations.
Finding and Applying for Scholarships (https://studentaid.gov/understand-aid/types/scholarships)

CollegeThoughts
Why College Thoughts? 20.4 million college students are enrolled in America's 4,140 US colleges: a sharp increase from the 11.7 million ten years ago. Now, more than ever, students need to enter the application process with a focused, self-directed plan. Good grades no longer guarantee admission to elite colleges and students need high quality assistance in navigating the rapidly shifting landscape. But with the average student only spending 38 minutes with their PUBLIC-SCHOOL guidance office during their high school years and a student: counselor ratio of 472:1 on average, you may be thinking that you will need a little extra help to achieve your goal in the college application process.
https://collegethoughts.com

The Manigault Institute
We teach an excellent and comprehensive SAT prep course for students applying to colleges. We have seen the SAT change over the past three decades and have altered our course to adapt to all of the changes, including teaching strategies to format math solutions without a calculator, answer more challenging reading comprehension questions, and teach grammar and editing techniques for writing.
https://manigaultinstitute.com/

A SHORT LISTING OF OPPORTUNITIES FOR STUDENTS

Experiment in International Living
Overseas opportunities for high school students. Due to Covid-19 virtual programs are available. In-country programs are on hold.
https://www.experiment.org/program-landing/destinations/

Congressional Awards for Young Americans
The Congressional Award is the United States Congress' award for young Americans. Our Foundation remains Congress' only charity. The program is non-partisan, voluntary, and non-competitive. Young people may register when they turn 13 1/2 years old and must complete their activities by their 24th birthday.
https://www.congressionalaward.org/program/

For a more complete listing of education and scholarship opportunities, please visit our website @
www.scholarshipstrategist.com

A NOTE FROM THE AUTHOR

It has been my absolute joy and honor to help not only my children but so many other children garner scholarships and entry into the best educational opportunities in the United States and abroad, and it is my sincere desire to help thousands more. The best education and opportunities should not be reserved for those most able to afford them, but for every child who when given the chance and the opportunity, will achieve beyond even their highest imagination!

Rhonda